FORAGING NEW ENGLAND

FORAGING NEW ENGLAND

Edible Wild Food and Medicinal Plants
from Maine to the Adirondacks to Long Island Sound

Second Edition

Tom Seymour

GUILFORD, CONNECTICUT
HELENA, MONTANA

AN IMPRINT OF GLOBE PEQUOT PRESS

FALCONGUIDES®

Copyright © 2002, 2013 by Morris Book Publishing, LLC

All photos by the author except where otherwise credited.

Map © Morris Book Publishing, LLC
Text design: Sheryl P. Kober
Project editors: Jennifer Kroll and Meredith Dias
Layout: Sue Murray

Seymour, Tom.
Foraging New England : edible wild food and medicinal plants from Maine to the Adirondacks to Long Island Sound / Tom Seymour. — Second edition.
    pages cm
Summary: "From beach peas to serviceberries, hen of the woods to Indian cucumber, ostrich ferns to sea rocket, Foraging New England guides the reader to the edible wild foods and healthful herbs of the Northeast. Helpfully organized by environmental zone, the book is an authoritative guide for nature lovers, outdoorsmen, and gastronomes."—Provided by publisher.
 Includes bibliographical references and index.
 ISBN 978-0-7627-7903-1 (pbk.)
1. Wild plants, Edible—New England—Identification. 2. Medicinal plants—New England—Identification. I. Title.
QK98.5.U6S49 2013
615.3'21—dc23

2012044057

Printed in the United States of America
10 9 8 7 6 5 4 3 2 1

To my maternal grandmother, Beatrice White

She had a love for nature and a sound knowledge of the healing powers of wild plants. Her memory is a constant inspiration for all who knew her.

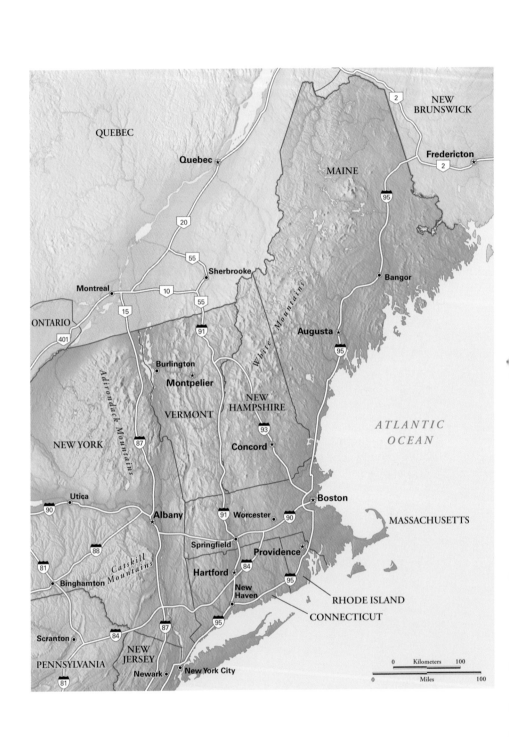

CONTENTS

PREFACE

Since release of the 2002 edition of *Foraging New England,* interest in foraging for wild plants has grown by several magnitudes. It was always my intent when the time came to add a number of plant species to a revised edition. My specialty is plants, and when speaking of foraging, plants immediately come to mind. But this revised edition also includes some freshwater and sea life.

I am very pleased to offer readers a number of new plants—the mainstay of the forager's diet and the main reason to go foraging. I hope those who are reading this book for the first time enjoy the time they spend locating, identifying, and harvesting the wild plants discussed in this book. And I sincerely hope that those who own the first edition of *Foraging New England* find that the additional plants described here will add a new and exciting dimension to their days afield. Good foraging.

ACKNOWLEDGMENTS

Special thanks go to Jeff Serena, former executive editor at Globe Pequot. It was he who saw the need for a regional foraging series and asked me to pen this book. A host of other persons have supported and assisted me in my ongoing love for foraging. Among these are my friend Ken Allen; my grandpa, Tom White; and my friends John and Eleanor Avener.

INTRODUCTION
New England, the Forager's Paradise

Mountains and hills, rivers and streams, tidal rivers and seashores: New England's diverse geography is representative of what the rest of the country has to offer. Sandy plains, more typical of the West, are found here too, as demonstrated in the vast "blueberry barrens" of Washington County, Maine. Deep swamps, as seemingly impenetrable as Southern bayous, brim with fascinating plants and animals.

New England winters are noted for their severity, but the cold and snow of winter have benefits that people too often fail to appreciate. For instance, many beautiful and useful plants drop seeds that need stratification: The seed must pass a season of below-freezing temperatures before it is ready to germinate when spring arrives. And even during the coldest, snowiest winters, the occasional balmy day lifts our spirits and calls us outside to check animal tracks in the snow while enjoying a hot cup of pine-needle tea.

New England springs have an ephemeral quality about them. We try our best to capture the essence of spring—to sample all it has to offer—before it escapes. The first warm day in March releases earthy scents from recently thawed hillsides—scents that have not teased our senses since the previous fall. The urge to go out and search on the south-facing side of the house for the first spindly, fragile dandelions is too strong to resist. Maple sap drips from broken branches, and insects, awakened from their long winter sleep, go about their business as if winter had never happened.

From spring through the first frosts of fall, New England offers a continually changing list of wild treasures. It is difficult for the forager to keep up with whatever is ready at the moment. Mostly we have our favorite species and take pains to be at the right place at the right time to harvest them; for the rest it is catch as catch can. New England literally has too much for the forager to sample in one lifetime.

Even those living in the northernmost section of New England are never much more than half a day's drive from the seashore. Here, on the sandbars, gravel, and rocks that make up the New England coast, are species that practically beg the forager to sample. The mountains, on the other hand, contain dozens of useful and interesting plant and animal species. Our rural New England roadsides have their own collection of edible and medicinal plants. Even in the largest cities, vacant lots don't remain vacant for long; plant invaders—usually desirable, edible species—quickly take up residence.

My idea of heaven on Earth goes something like this: Drive to the shore and pick a good assortment of whatever seaside veggies are in season. With the vegetable portion of the meal safely stowed, the next step is to gather about three pounds of blue mussels. The briny harvest is taken home, the mussels steamed and the vegetables stir-fried, and all is enjoyed outside under the shade of the huge, whispering white pines behind my little cottage. Kings, princes, and potentates may have the money to buy better fare, but truth to tell, where could they find better than the homey, free seaside meal just described? The forager's life is sprinkled with earthly pleasures.

Given all this, it is easy to see how New England and foraging go hand in hand. It really doesn't get any better than this!

Identifying Plants

While wild-plant harvesters need not be trained botanists, a basic knowledge of some of the more common terms used to describe plants is definitely in order. Plants do not retain the same physical features all season long. Some immature plants bear little resemblance to the adult or flowering plant. And yet certain traits are always present to set the plant apart from others and identify it. Shape of leaves and their arrangements, for instance, are important characteristics and must be considered in making a proper identification. Besides, wild plants have their dangers, and the only way to avoid using a toxic plant is to be absolutely assured of the plant's identification.

That aside, it's just plain fun to learn the basics of plant identification. To be unaware of the nature of the plants we see every day—to pass them by and not know their names, their uses, and their habits—is to live in a form of darkness. That darkness can easily be dispelled with a little study. The glossary in the back of this book will untangle the botanical terms necessary to identify wild plants.

Latin names are more specific and less ambiguous than common names and are very useful for identifying wild plants and animals. The system of Latin names we use today was developed centuries ago and still proves its worth. The Latin names of living things have two parts: genus and species. The first word in the name is the genus and refers to the wider group to which the plant or animal belongs. Evening primrose, for example, belongs to the genus *Oenothera*. The second term in the Latin name is the species. It tells us something special about the plant to identify it exactly. Evening primrose carries the species name *biennis,* which indicates that the plant is biennial: living for two years. Thus the Latin name of evening primrose is *Oenothera biennis,* sometimes abbreviated to *O. biennis.*

The Forager's Tools

Recreational foraging is almost virtuous in its simplicity. Specialized tools are definitely not needed, although a few basic hand tools—usually the common tools found in virtually every home workshop, barn, or garage—can make collecting easier. A typical recreational forager's arsenal of tools might include a hand trowel, jackknife, spade, and spading fork. And a pair of leather work gloves always comes in handy.

You'll need to take something afield to hold the bounty. My favorite container is a handmade brown ash basket. Cloth bags are also good. Plastic bags tend to make plants go limp, and paper bags don't hold up well when it's wet outside.

If nature presents an impromptu bounty and no container is available, the mark of a true forager is an innate ability to improvise. Once when I was pulling out of a parking lot in Bangor, Maine, my headlights illuminated a large patch of what appeared to be puffball mushrooms. A closer inspection proved that here, indeed, was a veritable bounty. But search as I might, I could find no container to hold the mushrooms.

It was a difficult situation. This place was an hour's drive from my house, too far to make it worthwhile to drive home and return in the daylight, armed with bags and baskets. But this wasn't my first time around the track. I finally remembered that I did have several suitable containers. Two spare jackets lay folded upon the backseat of my car. I could spread them out flat, pile the mushrooms on them, and then wrap them up like a package for the trip home. Soon two bulging jackets held a year's supply of fresh, tender puffballs. A true forager is always prepared. And when we are not prepared, we can always improvise!

Harvesting Techniques

Picking plant matter need not harm the plant. Even plants that are relatively scarce (not threatened or endangered but locally scarce) can be judiciously harvested without harm.

To harvest wild plants, always gather from a substantial group of plants, not from a small group of only a few individuals. Leaves, tender tips, and even stems can be snipped individually from one plant here, another plant there. This method actually encourages growth, just as pruning stimulates hearty growth on domestic plants.

Harvesting roots, tubers, or rhizomes is much the same. Rather than harm the plants, concentrating on extensive plant colonies will stimulate lush growth.

The best way for a beginner to proceed is to learn everything there is to know about one plant at a time. Learn it inside out, in all seasons. Then go on to the next plant. Proceed with caution and a desire to learn. That's all it takes to become a safe, happy, and satisfied forager.

Toxic Plants

Proper identification of all plants is critical. Did you know that some members of the parsley family are as lethal as the deadliest poison mushroom? It's true.

Even a small nibble of poison hemlock (*Conium maculatum*) can kill. Other plants, such as white baneberry (*Actaea pachypoda*), cause skin blistering and, when ingested, painful gastrointestinal difficulties. Still other plants alter the heartbeat and blood pressure. And the list goes on. Should this cause the forager to refrain from dealing with plants? Absolutely not. It should, though, be ample cause to consult a field guide before as much as touching an unfamiliar plant. Better yet, take the field guide, or several field guides, out on your foraging trips.

Mushrooms

"Mushrooming" is a popular, organized activity. Mushroom clubs abound in New England. After all, thanks to our moderate, often moist climate, our area is prime mushroom habitat. Nothing beats a field trip with a knowledgeable individual, and all it takes to find a group or club in the local area is to call the closest Extension Service. For those unfamiliar with the Extension Service, it offers education in the areas of agriculture and food, home and family, the environment, community economic development, and youth, typically through a local university.

Poison Ivy, Biting Bugs, and Other Things to Watch For

"Leaves of three, let it be" run the words to a well-known verse. Poison ivy and to a lesser extent virgin's bower, or wild clematis, have three divided leaflets, occur in New England, and are responsible for untold suffering, mostly in the form of severe skin irritation. Poison ivy is sometimes difficult to recognize because its appearance varies. Virgin's bower, while common and growing in dense colonies, is a climbing vine. Often the unwary don't recognize it for what it is; thus the value of the before-mentioned verse.

So how do casual visitors to the fields and woods manage to keep away from poison ivy and virgin's bower? The first and safest course is to stay on open paths and avoid coming into contact with any plants. But foraging requires some intimate contact with the green countryside, so the next best safeguard is to wear long-sleeved shirts and long pants and to bathe thoroughly upon returning home. Generally this is enough to thwart any problems resulting from casual contact with poison plants. Jewelweed—which grows nearly everywhere and is described in this volume—is not only a good prophylactic but also has properties that will soon dispel any rash that occurs, along with its accompanying discomfort.

Long pants and long-sleeved shirts are also good protection against biting insects, which are legion in New England. An insect repellent containing DEET (diethyltoluamide) won't keep bugs from buzzing, but it will prevent insects from biting. In some instances repellents containing DEET can cause allergic-type reactions. This is true in my own case, although in my opinion coughing and sneezing are less troubling than insect bites, which can become infected.

Those who are sensitive to DEET have little choice but to wear protective netting. The so-called "green" insect repellents containing citronella and pennyroyal do little to prevent insects from biting, at least in my experience.

Deer ticks spread Lyme disease, a debilitating disease that is often difficult to diagnose. Again, try to stay on open trails as much as possible and wear long pants and long-sleeved shirts.

Bees can be a real problem. It is relatively easy to spot a paper wasp or hornet nest high in a tree. It is practically impossible to spot a yellow jacket nest, though. These mean critters have 1-inch-diameter escape and entrance holes in the ground, often at the base of a tree or shrub. Late summer and fall are the most dangerous times for these aggressive creatures. Not only are they more apt to swarm on a defenseless forager at that time, but my experience shows that they deliver a larger dose of venom too. People who are allergic to bee stings must be vigilant. The only defense we have is to watch for yellow jackets entering and exiting—and be sure we don't poke around the ground where any suspect hole exists.

Spiders are another story. These creatures lurk in dark places, crevices, corners, nooks, and crannies. Not much can be done to keep spiders from biting except to look first before inserting your hands or fingers in dark areas. Spiders are as much a threat in the home and garden as they are in the fields and forests. Even cold weather does not diminish the chance of an encounter. Once while ice fishing on a particularly cold and windy day, the wind swept a large, and very much alive, spider across the ice in front of me.

Venomous snakes are present in New England, except for Maine. However, these are pit vipers (copperheads and rattlesnakes) and hunt mostly at night. In states other than Maine, it is good policy to watch where you put your hands when climbing in ledgy areas and to scan the trail ahead of you for snakes. Generally snakes are not a threat to foragers who exercise normal caution. In fact, pit vipers are scarce and in need of protection; if you sight one, please leave it be.

Weather

Thunder and lightning signal danger. As soon as you hear distant thunder, it is time to quit foraging and head for safety. Do not stand near any tall, solitary tree, and do not stand in the open. A motor vehicle is relatively safe because lightning currents are carried mostly on the vehicle's outer surface and then go to ground; just don't touch any metal parts. Lightning is a very real threat, not just in New England but everywhere.

Giardia

In addition to the possible toxic side effects of eating wild plants, a word about giardiasis, commonly called giardia, is in order. Giardia is an infection of the small intestine caused by the *Giardia lamblia* protozoan. Contaminated water is the culprit; beavers (giardia is also known as "beaver fever") and muskrats are carriers, and raw sewage leaching into waterways also tends to spread the protozoan. Drinking suspect water is always dangerous, but giardia can also be spread by other means. I believe that a certain danger exists when consuming aquatic plant matter from suspect water. Because of this threat, rinse plants thoroughly in clean water before eating them.

Medicinal Plants

It is greatly rewarding to go outside and pluck a plant, take it inside, steep it in water, drink the resulting tea, and gain relief from minor discomforts. It is dangerous, however, to consider plant medicines as anything but gentle helpers for minor complaints. Failure to consult qualified medicinal practitioners can lead to more severe illness or even death.

Private Land

Although the world is "our blueberry," we foragers must operate within certain bounds. It is unlawful to forage upon land owned by another without permission. Additionally, some public lands prohibit picking any plant matter. It is therefore imperative that you consult local regulations before picking any plant or capturing any animal. You must always secure permission when venturing upon private lands. To those who would say, "But I know the landowner isn't going to pick this stuff, so I might as well," I can only reply: "Nonetheless, we must still secure permission beforehand. Not only does common courtesy demand it, but it is also the law."

Environmental Cautions

Amphibians, plants, reptiles, and insects all share a common thread: Many of them are endangered, threatened, or of special concern. Fortunately the current trend toward appreciation of nature and the desire to learn more about the natural world has illuminated the plight of these living creatures.

Foragers are in an enviable position: They are outdoors throughout the different seasons and so can observe the status of the creatures and plants in their own circle of travel. Their observations contribute to our knowledge of formerly little-known creatures and plants. Organizations such as FrogWatch USA (details are given in the entry on bullfrogs; see page 213) gather data on amphibians from amateur naturalists. And hometown newspapers throughout New England now run nature columns, written by professional and amateur naturalists who outline important environmental issues.

As we become involved in nature, we become more a part of it and begin to work with, not against, it. Being environmentally responsible requires commitment. Foragers are at the forefront of the national awakening to the importance of our natural world and all the creatures that swim, fly, walk, creep, and crawl in and on it.

Seasons

Spring, summer, and fall are times of great activity for the forager. From the day in March when the first tender, green shoot pokes out from the forest litter to fall, when the last killing frost draws a distinct and final close to the growing season, foragers have more to do, learn, and observe than they have time for. Each season brings its own delights, joys, and bounty.

It is important for foragers to understand the concept of what I call "mini seasons." Nothing remains the same in nature for more than a brief, fleeting instant. Plants do not appear the same from one month to the next. And each plant has its prime time for harvest or appreciation. The four seasons can therefore be divided up into lots of brief segments, or mini seasons.

For example, even before the ground is fully thawed in spring, the evening primrose is present along dirt roads and gravel lanes, ready for harvest. The flat, basal rosettes of the plant are—at that time and for that short time only—good

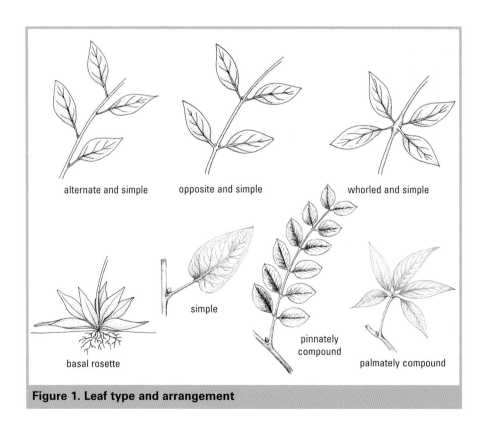

alternate and simple   opposite and simple   whorled and simple

basal rosette   simple   pinnately compound   palmately compound

Figure 1. Leaf type and arrangement

for use in salads or as cooked vegetables. The roots too are edible, again only for a short period. When the warm rays of the spring sun cause the outspread leaves to pick up and reach for the sky, the root becomes pithy and inedible and the leaves become tough. In late summer and early fall, the blooming plant bears little resemblance to the small, green-and-red-tinted bunch of tender leaves seen along the roadside in early spring.

The evening primrose points out the value of recognizing the mini seasons. Each of these tiny slices of time can be recognized by the state of the various wild plants. Other factors contribute to the mini seasons. Spring peepers, wood frogs, and common toads can be heard at night, calling in the swamps and wetlands. This too lasts for only a brief interval. Bird arrivals—the warbler migration in particular—come on fast and are soon over, many of the birds having only stopped for a few days on their way north. Knowing the signs of the seasons contributes greatly to the forager's enjoyment and appreciation of nature.

Finally, winter is the time to relax, study, read books, and enjoy the wild harvest. Common dandelions never taste better than when nor'easters howl and roads are plugged with snow. A cup of herbal tea made with foraged plant leaves or flowers imparts a warm glow to the spirit. Medicinal plants, dried and safely stored, are ready to combat the simple cold. By these means the forager has managed to save a bit of the previous season. This is what helps us bear up until the following spring, when that first wood frog heralds the new season and a renewal of life.

Plants of the Seashore

The New England shore is home to a wide variety of edible plants and animals. And strange as it may seem, edible seaweeds cannot be listed among the numbers of easily gathered foodstuffs; most of these are available only along the Bold Coast of Maine, where depths plunge precipitously. A boat is usually necessary to gather edible seaweed, and even then it's not convenient except during extreme low tides. But a host of other ready-at-hand foods exist to delight and tantalize any forager willing to learn the ways of the seashore. Even better, the seaside plants grow not only on the actual coast but along tidal rivers and streams as well. A forager can find good pickings almost anyplace the tide rises and falls.

The well-defined line of demarcation between the shore and the inland zones is of great interest to the forager. Plants that only grow inland are found scant inches from the extreme high-tide zone, and plants that only grow where they can be touched by sea spray grow tantalizingly close to the upper extremes of the beach. In New England our planting zones, as illustrated in the seed catalogs, are often vague, but the seashore and the inland zones are practically carved in stone. The best of both worlds can be found here side by side.

Seaside foragers need to be aware of one caveat: Many of our more popular beaches have become favorite spots for people to walk their dogs. Given what dogs are fond of doing on plants, it may be advisable to limit wild-food gathering to the more secluded stretches of seashore.

GOOSE TONGUE
Plantago juncoides

Synonyms: Seaside plantain, shore greens
Uses: Cooked vegetable, salad ingredient
Range: Seashores throughout New England
Similarity to toxic species: Goose tongue has a vague similarity to arrowgrass (*Triglochin maritima*). Differences are considerable, however. The leaves of arrowgrass are fairly thin, whereas those of goose tongue are much wider and softer. And the succulent-like goose tongue leaves have an obvious groove. The straight leaves of arrowgrass are primarily upright, while goose tongue leaves are sometimes twisted at crazy angles and tend to droop; often a few leaves are prostrate. Arrowgrass is primarily a threat to cud-chewing animals.
Best time: Late May through August
Status: Common
Tools needed: None

Goose tongue is related to the common plantain (see page 185). The difference between the two is in the leaves: Common plantain has wide leaves with prominent veins; goose tongue has slender, fleshy leaves. Also, goose tongue leaves have a deep indentation their entire length. A cross section of one of the 4- to 8-inch leaves would look like the cross section of a common house gutter. The seed stalk is shorter than that of the common plantain, rarely exceeding 10 inches. Goose tongue usually grows in dense colonies, ranging from slightly below to slightly above the high-tide line. Sometimes, especially on rocky, inhospitable shores, goose tongue plants grow singly.

FORAGER NOTE: Goose tongue cooks quickly. It can be steamed or boiled.

Goose tongue gets its name, naturally enough, from its similarity in appearance to a slender, pointed goose's tongue. Anyone who has ever been chased by an angry goose (it happens) will note the likeness.

Goose tongue is one of those plants that are common, widespread, and yet go unnoticed by the vast majority of visitors to the seashore. Once goose tongue was a New England favorite, ranking in popularity with dandelions and fiddleheads. But over the past fifty years or so, the folks who favored this ubiquitous seaside vegetable have passed on and few, if any, have stepped in to perpetuate the tradition of walking to the shore to pick a "mess of shore greens." The paucity of adherents, however, has no bearing on the goodness or worth of this flavorful plant. Indeed, goose tongue is sweet and mild, with just a trace of saltiness.

RECIPES

When boiling goose tongue, use a scant amount of water; the leaves need not be covered. Boiling any green this way is similar to steaming in a commercially manufactured food steamer. Once the leaves darken (the same way some green beans darken when cooked) and become limp, drain the greens and serve. A bit of butter and a lick of ground pepper go well with goose tongue. Some enjoy a dash of cider vinegar. My suggestion is to sample the greens first, sans vinegar, and then, if desired, try a splash of vinegar. Watch the salt, though. Even after thorough rinsing in freshwater (a must for all greens, especially those from the seashore), goose tongue retains a slight salty taste.

Some people like their shore greens in a salad, either in addition to other ingredients or as the main ingredient. Either way, the leaves should be chopped first. The easiest way to accomplish this is to use scissors, as when cutting chives.

Although goose tongue is common and abundant, it won't remain so if we harvest it indiscriminately. The trick is not to pull the plant up by its roots. Instead, trim the individual leaves. This is easily accomplished by snapping them with thumb and forefinger, like a fresh, crisp green bean. And it's good policy to take only the largest leaves, leaving the smaller leaves to grow and sustain the plant.

Not everyone has my good fortune to live so near the seashore. My grocery shopping sometimes consists of a visit to the store for bread and staples and a stop at the local goose tongue bed on the way home. Steamed goose tongue, along with whatever is in season in my vegetable garden, is a common summertime meal at my place.

FREEZING

Goose tongue makes a superior frozen vegetable. Blanch the greens in boiling water, drain, and immediately drop them in ice-cold water to cool. When thoroughly cooled, drain the greens again, put them in freezer bags, and the job is completed. Frozen goose tongue easily lasts a full year in the freezer. It pleases me to no end to sit in my tiny kitchen and watch the nor'easters howl outside while I dine on steamed goose tongue. I can think of no finer way to re-create the essence of summer!

ORACHE
Atriplex patula

Uses: Cooked vegetable, salad ingredient
Range: Widespread above the high-tide line along the entire New England seacoast
Similarity to toxic species: None
Best time: June through September
Status: Common and plentiful
Tools needed: None

A member of the goosefoot family, orache is a generally symmetrical, bushy plant—although sometimes plants growing in shade or on windswept, bare spots are scrawny and prostrate. Orache can grow to 2 feet in height, and the leaves are the key to identification. Roughly similar to leaves of lamb's-quarters (see page 44), orache leaves have fewer teeth. In essence the leaf is shaped like an arrowhead, with the "barbs" pointing out to the side. The leaf, especially the bottom, is coated with a grainy-feeling powder that can be wiped off with the fingers. The insignificant flowers grow in the leaf axils.

Orache leaves are easily stirred into motion by the slightest sea breeze when, like quaking aspens, they expose their light-colored undersides. This habit makes them easy to identify, even from a great distance. Of all the wild seaside

FORAGER NOTE: Wild vegetables should be carefully tended, just like fresh fish, from the time they are gathered until they reach the table.

Pick the leaves and tender stem tips, rinse, and drop in a little boiling water. Cook until the orache becomes dark, like spinach. Use plenty of fresh orache to begin with—it loses its bulk in cooking. Drain well and serve with butter, salt, and ground black pepper.

vegetables, orache is the most dependable; it is literally everywhere, no matter if the beach is rocky or muddy, gravelly or smooth.

Orache prefers the immediate high-tide line, often growing among, around, and through the various clumps of driftwood, dried seaweed, and other types of flotsam found there. No seaborne material, no matter how dense, seems able to smother the hardy and determined orache.

A handmade brown ash basket is my favorite container when picking orache. Placing the leaves and tender tips (the stems are edible too, as long as they are tender and thin) in a bag seems to compact them, making them more difficult to separate for rinsing later. If the weather is hot and humid, my orache leaves go into an ice-filled cooler upon returning to the car.

Orache has a sweetness akin to the most tender young spinach, but with none of the strong aftertaste. Orache does, however, have a distinctly ethereal dimension to its flavor—something best appreciated in the manner of a wine taster sipping the wine and then breathing through the nose. Take one forkful of orache, slowly chew and swallow, and, before taking another bite, examine the flavor sensed on the back of the tongue.

Orache is a big hit with participants in my seaside wild-plant walks. We usually try to pick and identify enough plants to provide a wild-food meal upon returning to my place. Orache, being the most abundant, yields an immediate reward for the first-time forager. It is easy to pick a basket- or bagful in short order. And though everything is new and different to most of these folks, it is the orache that elicits the most comments at the end of the meal.

Some years ago a local plant company offered orache seeds in its annual catalog. Although this wasn't exactly the same orache as grows by the sea, the company included a glowing description of the sweet flavor. It seemed a good idea to try and grow this cultivated orache at home and circumvent the short drive to the seashore. But the stuff didn't grow well, was highly prone to insect infestation, and, most important, didn't taste nearly as good as the "real thing." Sometimes we really can't improve on nature.

FREEZING

Orache freezes well. Blanch, cool, drain, and place in plastic bags for freezing. No store-bought frozen vegetable can compare.

RECIPE

Try cider vinegar on steamed or boiled orache, though it tends to cover up the fine flavor of the plant.

SEA BLITE
Suaeda maritima

Uses: Trail nibble, cooked vegetable, salad ingredient
Range: Entire New England seashore, near the high-tide line
Similarity to toxic species: None
Best time: June through August
Status: Common and abundant
Tools needed: None

Drifts of bluish-green sea blite dot the upper reaches of most beaches. A member of the goosefoot family, sea blite can live in gravel, in sand, and even among rocks and boulders. A spreading plant, soft and vine-like, sea blite rarely stands more than 1 foot tall. More often the individual branches hug the ground. The tiny, alternate leaves are round and pointed, reminding the landlubber of any of

RECIPE

A bit of chopped sea blite adds an interesting, pleasant dimension to any salad. Rinse, cut into small bits with kitchen shears, and sprinkle over the salad.

the various species of spruce. But unlike spruce, sea blite is not prickly. Instead it is soft and tender, succulent-like. Sea blite has tiny yellowish-green flowers tucked in the leaf axils.

Most foragers like their sea blite boiled or steamed. While it is indeed a fine potherb, it has several other uses that should not be overlooked.

Sea blite is easily picked by snapping the vine-like branches with your fingers. By picking only a few sprigs from each plant, it is possible to impart a manicured look to the plants without doing any harm whatsoever. Be sure not to pull sea blite up by its roots.

🌿 Trail food: *Sea blite is a superior trail nibble. The tender tips, stems, and leaves are great to chew on while walking the beach, searching for other seaside edibles. Sea blite is quite salty, especially raw. But it isn't as salty as salted peanuts, potato chips, or any of the popular jerky products. And salt in sea blite, being sea salt, is full of important trace elements, as opposed to common table salt, which may or may not contain only added iodine.*

RECIPE

Rinsed, chopped sea blite makes a perfectly good boiled vegetable. It cooks fully in about ten minutes. Some authorities recommend cooking in two waters (boiling twice) to remove the salty taste. That salty taste, though, is what makes sea blite stand out among the seaside vegetables. Circumventing the salt taste is kind of like cooking rhubarb stalks with so much sugar that none of the tart, mouth-puckering flavor remains. It is the tartness, after all, that makes rhubarb unique. And so it is with sea blite—salt fanciers take note.

EXTRA RECIPE

My favorite use of sea blite is in a seaside stir-fry. Used alone or with any of the seaside edible plants mentioned here, sea blite comes alive in a hot wok. The ratio of one plant to another is entirely a matter of personal choice and, of course, availability. No matter. Some things are best when not reduced to ounces, cups, or teaspoons. The pure off-the-cuff seaside stir-fry is a thing of beauty, a one-of-a-kind work of art.

BEACH PEA
Lathyrus japonicus

Uses: Trail nibble, cooked vegetable
Range: Widespread along the entire New England coast, slightly above the high-tide line
Similarity to toxic species: Beach pea bears a slight resemblance to vetchling (*L. palustris*). Vetchling generally, but not always, has a winged stem, as does its relative, that favorite shrub of landscapers, euonymus. The beach pea is easy to differentiate from other members of the *Lathyrus* genus, however, because it produces peas in pods that are identical in every way to cultivated peas except that they are tiny.
Best time: June and July
Status: Common and widespread
Tools needed: None

The beach pea is a vining plant, with leaves that can be either opposite or alternate. In my part of Maine, most beach peas have opposite leaves and are easily identified because the leaves, rather than splaying out, are held up, nearly touching each other. The showy, pealike flowers range in color from purple to pink to violet. The fruits are borne in seedpods that look like miniature garden pea pods.

Beach peas are at their peak of ripeness for only a short time. Sometimes it takes many trips to the beach pea bed to determine when the peas will be ripe.

And as often as not, something comes up; our nonforaging lives interfere, and by the time we return to pick the beach peas, they are gone by, tough and insipid.

FORAGER NOTE: Because beach peas lose some of their sweetness when cool, it is best to serve them hot.

But that is what makes them so hauntingly desirable.

Barring the luxury of being able to visit the beach pea stand periodically, it helps to keep records, much as canny gardeners keep track of the first and last frosts, when the first tomato comes off ripe, and when the first mess of peas is ready. But the seasons in New England are notorious for being unpredictable. And unpredictable is a fit term to describe beach peas.

For all that, beach peas have another trait that makes them less than popular among visitors to the seashore: The individual peas are so tiny, it takes an unduly long time to shell enough for a good meal. That said, it is important to remember that the more effort a project requires, the more the finished product is appreciated.

Beach peas impress me with their tenacity. One of my old favorite beach pea stands is on a rocky, windswept slope. Here the pea vines twine around huge boulders and among giant timbers from long-forgotten piers that succumbed to some ancient hurricane. How anything can thrive in this repressive environment is beyond me. But the beach peas do. What's more, they seem to like it!

Once, the youngsters in our foraging group became enthralled with beach peas. The peas, happily, were at the peak of perfection, and the kids picked a colossal bunch. We adults made it clear that it would be their job to shell the peas upon returning home. Surprisingly the children tackled the job and stuck to it like troupers, without complaining once. When the full wild meal was served, the kids got first crack at the boiled beach peas. I'm sure they were no better than any other peas these youngsters had tasted, but their hands-on experience made all the difference in the world. What a great lesson in cause and effect and the value of diligence.

RECIPE

When preparing a complex meal, save the beach peas for last. When everything is nearly done, pour the shelled peas into boiling water and cook for about ten minutes. Serve immediately.

Trail food: *At the height of ripeness, fresh beach peas are pretty good raw, as trail nibbles. When past their prime, however, and the pods turn yellow and are tinted with red streaks, the peas become tough and insipid, better suited as ammo for peashooters than table fare.*

Beach peas can be frozen, but why bother? Take my advice and eat beach peas fresh, on the day they are picked. Then they can become part of an annual ritual, the beach pea feast. Little things like this are all-important pieces in the great puzzle that is the forager's year.

SEA-ROCKET
Cakile edentula

Uses: Trail nibble, salad ingredient, cooked vegetable
Range: Widespread at or above the high-tide line along most of the Atlantic coast, including all of New England
Similarity to toxic species: None
Best time: June through August
Status: Common and plentiful
Tools needed: None

Sea-rocket, a member of the mustard family, is found just above the high-tide line. Its sprawling habit, as well as its dark green, fleshy leaves and succulent stems, make identification easy.

RECIPE

Besides nibbling the tender stems, terminal ends, buds, flowers, and seedpods straight from the plant, sea-rocket can be finely cut and added to salads. Using only a small amount will impart a flavor that is well defined yet not overpowering. Uninitiated guests may wonder, but they will never guess the source of this clean, interesting flavor.

The shiny, smooth, leathery-looking leaves have irregular, coarse teeth with few if any sharp edges. The tiny purple or blue flowers have four petals, each one cleft at the end. They appear in summer, followed by the distinct, two-parted seedpods that mark the beginning of the end of the season for this estimable seaside plant.

That sea-rocket is one of the mustards is made convincingly evident by its piquant taste. This sharp flavor is not at all unlike the hot mustard paste served in Asian restaurants, which is why those who enjoy hot mustard should make every effort to become acquainted with sea-rocket. Those who dislike mustard are advised to give the plant a wide berth.

Trail food: *As a trail nibble (for mustard lovers, that is), sea-rocket excels. It ranks high among my favorites. My fondness for fresh sea-rocket is such that my passing along the beach can be marked by the destruction wreaked on the youngest and most tender sea-rocket plants. I have found that too much sea-rocket can trigger mild indigestion. That's a small price, though, for such a heady indulgence.*

GLASSWORT
Salicornia spp.

Uses: Trail nibble, salad ingredient, cooked vegetable
Range: Widespread along the New England seacoast, tidal rivers, and streams
Similarity to toxic species: None
Best time: June through September
Status: Common
Tools needed: None

Glasswort grows in dense colonies, always where it can be touched by extreme high tide and sometimes where it is regularly immersed. A member of the goosefoot family, glasswort is interesting to observe throughout the growing season because the change in appearance as the plant matures is so dramatic. As opposed to, say, a tomato—which even as a seedling has all the characteristics of an adult—immature glasswort plants resemble single, naked nubs. As the season progresses, glasswort (remember that since glasswort grows in massive colonies, the change is not so much a singular event as it

FORAGER NOTE: Foragers wishing to indoctrinate others into the myriad pleasures of foraging should select glasswort as the initial wild plant. No one in my experience has ever responded in other than a positive manner when first sampling glasswort.

is a mass occurrence) gains height as it sprouts branches. The overall effect is like a bed of moss slowly transforming into a forest of fir trees. And while early in the season glasswort sports shades of brilliant lime green, toward the end of summer the shading turns to olive drab and, finally, to orange.

The two glassworts of most value to New England foragers are dwarf glasswort (*S. bigelovii*) and slender glasswort (*S. europaea*). The differences between the two are that dwarf glasswort branches are relatively short and stubby, while slender glasswort has longer, more slender branches. Note that some plants may never develop branches, remaining as solitary, slender spikes the entire season. Glasswort flowers, which grow in the axils (or joints) of the plant, are tiny and hardly noticeable.

A third variety, woody glasswort (*S. virginica*), exists in southern New England, but the dwarf and slender types are better suited to the forager's needs. In northern New England the forager is more likely to encounter the dwarf variety.

To my mind, glasswort is a dinosaur, primitive and ancient. But my fascination with this weird-looking plant doesn't end with its physical characteristics. Its salty-sweet flavor beckons me to stop, find a comfortable place to sit or recline, and graze for a while.

Trail food: *Glasswort is utterly delicious raw. The serious nibbler should select the most tender tips and branches. These are quite brittle and snap easily between thumb and forefinger.*

RECIPE

Nibble the fresh plant at the seashore, and pick some more to take home for a salad. The salad may be entirely composed of glasswort, or the glasswort may be mixed with other seaside goodies. Consider a combination of sea blite, glasswort, sea-rocket, orache, and goose tongue. Sprinkled with some balsamic vinegar and topped with freshly ground black pepper, this seaside potpourri could make you a legendary forager in your own time!

EXTRA RECIPE

Cook glasswort for ten minutes and serve as a hot vegetable.

SILVERWEED
Potentilla anserina

Uses: Trail nibble, cooked vegetable
Range: Common locally throughout New England; silverweed prefers rocky, gravelly shores, at or somewhat below the high-tide line.
Similarity to toxic species: Silverweed leaves bear a slight resemblance to tansy, which contains a toxic oil. The forager should encounter no difficulties in identification, though, because tansy is an upright plant, while silverweed bears prostrate stems.
Best time: July through September
Status: Common
Tools needed: While the edible roots can be harvested by digging with the fingers, a garden trowel or three-pronged, handheld weeder is recommended.

Silverweed, a member of the rose family, sports leaves that are silvery underneath. They are divided, with coarse, sharp-toothed leaflets that grow opposite each other, with the larger leaflets on top and the smaller near the base. The yellow flowers have five petals. The white roots are shiny and fleshy.

The silverweed on my local seashore grows in the most difficult areas to harvest: the sharp gravel between rocks and boulders. This is not so everywhere, thankfully. Still, given my situation, a handful of silverweed roots harvested with the hands represents lots of hard work. It seems I never remember to carry a digging tool.

Oddly, historical reference to coastal residents eating silverweed is lacking. None of the old-timers of my acquaintance even seem to know what silverweed is. Here, then, is a "new" plant for today's forager. Enjoy!

🌿 Trail food: *Because of the difficulty (for me) involved in harvesting a good supply of silverweed root, I have become accustomed to eating it raw. The crisp texture and sweet flavor make it a favorite trail nibble. Nobody else, so far as I know, eats raw silverweed roots. That is their loss. My motto is, "If it tastes good raw, eat it raw."*

RECIPE

Boil the starchy roots for up to twenty minutes before serving. Salt, pepper, and butter complement this vegetable. And despite my preference for raw silverweed roots, the cooked product is delicious and well worth the effort involved.

NORTHERN BAY
Myrica pensylvanica

Uses: Spice, flavor additive
Range: Northern bay is found throughout New England, rarely more than a mile from the coast and often at the water's edge. It prefers infertile soil.
Similarity to toxic species: None
Best time: June through September
Status: Common and abundant
Tools needed: None

Before writing this entry, I sat down to a hearty ham and lima bean soup, seasoned with northern bay leaves. The leaves were picked last summer, dried, and stored in a glass jar in my cupboard. Now, fortified with the essence of that noble spice, it seems proper to write about it.

Hardly a schoolchild lives who hasn't heard of how the early colonists made candles from bayberry wax. The bay also yielded soap to our early

FORAGER NOTE: Don't store bay leaves in plastic bags; it could cause the leaves to sweat and lose some of their essential oil—and with it, much of their flavor.

settlers—bay wax saponifies well, making a fine soap. Interestingly, little if anything is recorded in the history books about the culinary aspects of northern bay.

Although northern bay, a member of the wax myrtle family, rarely grows more than 10 feet tall, certain venerable specimens attain heights of better than 20 feet. The so-called berries (really nutlets) are coated with a bluish-white, aromatic wax and should not be eaten. Instead, it is the leaves that are edible. These average between 2 and 3 inches long and are shiny on both sides, especially on the upper surface. In fact, they are so shiny that in order to photograph a bay shrub in full sunlight, you need to use a polarizer to cut the glare. The leaves have a few shallow indentations, or notches, near the end that give a slightly toothed appearance. Also, the leaves are broader at the end than at the base. The overall impression anyone has upon seeing a northern bay shrub for the first time is "dense and bushy."

Sometimes while walking along the shore, I like to take a handful of northern bay leaves, crush them in my hand, and savor the penetrating aroma. This lifts my spirits on those low-pressure days when fog hangs thick and dreary on the New England coast.

The leaves can be picked anytime they're large enough to bother with. You can easily pluck a pint or so of the stiff, shiny leaves in a few minutes. The leaves should be placed in a paper or cloth bag for the trip home.

FORAGER NOTE: Never crumple bay leaves before using.

Northern bay leaves are not the same as commercially available bay leaves, and they don't taste exactly the same either. Truthfully, the wild northern bay has a far superior flavor to the store-bought product. And if the price of commercial bay leaves were figured to the pound, they would surely be more expensive than the most precious metals. Northern bay is free.

Although northern bay occurs naturally within earshot of the sea, it can grow almost anywhere it is planted, as long as the ground is poor. In fact, while perusing a garden catalog, I was amused to see northern bay plants for sale. These cost about seven bucks per shrub. For those who don't have access to the shore, $7 seems a small-enough investment to ensure a steady supply of northern bay leaves.

DRYING

The leaves must be thoroughly dried before storing in a glass jar. My favorite method is to line the bottom of my trusty old brown ash basket with bay leaves and hang it on one of the cut nails driven into the beam that extends across my kitchen ceiling. The main thing, however accomplished, is to slow-dry the leaves in the cool shade. When they are brittle, they are ready to go into permanent storage in the spice closet. Be careful not to break the leaves when filling the storage container.

RECIPE

Dried northern bay leaves can be used in all manner of soups and stews. Add a few leaves to blue mussels prior to steaming and even to the water that lobsters will be steamed in. When making pickled mussels or pickled periwinkles, insert three or four northern bay leaves between the meats and the side of the canning jar. The list of uses is limited only by your imagination. Remember, though, to use the leaves whole and discard them after cooking. The spent leaf is tough and bland. The flavor will by then have been transferred from the leaf to the food.

WRINKLED ROSE
Rosa rugosa

Uses: Survival food, salad ingredient, nutritious tea
Range: Throughout New England, especially along the immediate seashore
Similarity to toxic species: None
Best time: August and September
Status: Common and abundant
Tools needed: None

Wrinkled rose flowers vary in color from white to pink to carmine. Each flower has five petals. The compound leaves have wrinkled leaflets, and the stems bristle with stiff hairs and sharp, needlelike thorns. Wrinkled rose often grows in

> ### RECIPE
>
> A powerful, vitamin C–laden tea can be made from the fresh or dried hips. Again, the hips should be split and the seeds and inner pulp discarded. Some honey dispels the inherent astringency, and the tea tastes pretty good besides being good for you.

company with the pasture, or wild, rose (*R. carolina*). The wild rose lacks the bristly hairs on the stem, but it does have thorns. Wild rose petals are pink.

Here in New England, reminders of our seafaring heritage are never farther than the nearest beach. The rugosa rose is one such reminder. These hardy plants literally grow everywhere along the seashore. Soil type, sun, or shade—nothing deters this tenacious Asian immigrant. It is said that the old sea captains, many of whose homes still stand, were the first to carry the seed-laden hips of

FORAGER NOTE: As a survival food, rose hips can't be equaled. These tart fruits are one of the world's most potent sources of vitamin C. I have not had to resort to rose hips myself and don't have any close friends who have. However, given their abundance and high vitamin content as well as their long season (they hang on the bushes all winter), they make a perfect survival food.

the wrinkled rose home to New England. The old-timers were fascinated with the flora and fauna of foreign lands, and they often carried seeds, plants, and whatnot back to New England. A certain awe strikes me every time I view vast sections of seaside banks literally covered with roses that almost certainly are descendants of those brought here by some long-forgotten seafarer.

The flowers themselves are plebeian when compared to modern hybrid roses, but they have much to offer. What seaside picnic isn't enhanced by a bouquet of such ancient and honorable blooms, picked fresh and stuck in whatever container the sea may have to offer? These unkempt roses of our beaches and seashores may be simple, but they own a certain dignity.

There are mountains of recipes for rose hips and petals, most of them time-consuming. Yet wrinkled rose, pasture rose, indeed all the roses, have some simple, basic uses that everyone should have at least a passing acquaintance with. First in line must be the use of rose hips as survival food.

Rose hips are really the fruiting bodies of the rose. These contain lots of small seeds and a fleshy, inner pulp. The skin of rose hips is tough and inedible. Some

RECIPE

The rose petals are edible. Nibble them raw, sprinkle them on salads, or use them as a garnish for meat dishes. Use your imagination.

foragers consider rose hips to be a passable trail nibble; I don't. The hips must be split, the seeds and soft pulp discarded, and the more substantial remaining pulp eaten. But no matter how many times I try, I find the flavor reminiscent of chewing on a vitamin C tablet—a little too astringent for my taste. We might say "A rose is a rose is a rose," but here in New England there's more to the story.

DRYING

After splitting and removing the seeds, rose hips can be dried on a rack with a nylon screen or simply placed in a basket hung in a cool, airy location.

Plants of Fertile Streamsides

Fertile streamsides, also known as the alluvial plain, are places of great richness and diverse plant life. The reason for this wonderful fertility may be illustrated by considering any of the world's great rivers. During its annual floods, the Nile deposits nutrient-rich silt and other matter along its banks, ensuring healthy and bountiful crops for farmers who understand and benefit from this endless cycle. And so it is with our New England streams, brooks, and rivers, albeit on a considerably smaller scale.

Certain plants require this rich, nutrient-laden ground and are rarely found in any other environment. Among these are ostrich ferns, stinging nettles, and wild oats. Several species of dock are usually found here, although they sometimes grow in drier conditions, as long as the ground is fertile.

In early spring the alluvial plain resembles a disaster zone. Signs of the recent snowmelt, with its accompanying high water and floods, are everywhere. Bits of dead grass, carried by the torrents and stuck on tree limbs many feet above the ground, wave forlornly in the gentle breeze. Dead trees, limbs akimbo, perhaps brought from far upstream, make walking difficult. And everywhere is a thin layer of damp but friable silt, the stuff that nature uses to replenish the soil and sustain and nourish streamside plant life.

As the sun warms the soil, the wild plants awaken, peeping through the streamside litter, beckoning the forager to come and partake. This is surely a good time to be alive and poking around in the New England outdoors. It's a brief season, but a glorious one.

GROUNDNUT
Apios americana

Synonym: Indian potato
Use: Root vegetable; use boiled or fried, but never raw
Range: Riparian habitat along streams and rivers throughout New England
Similarity to toxic species: None
Best time: Very early spring through late fall
Status: Common and abundant
Tools needed: Can be harvested by hand in early spring; otherwise, use a hand trowel or spading fork

Walnuts on a string, covered with coconut fiber—that pretty well describes a bunch of groundnuts, connected to one another via a string-like root. Groundnuts are tubers, the same as many root vegetables. A single groundnut, planted or otherwise deposited along some meandering stream, will soon send out roots and begin a new colony of groundnuts.

Groundnuts average about the size of a walnut, but some can grow to twice that and others are much smaller. The lucky forager may find as many as six or more tubers attached to one root. Some groundnuts have an overall globular, or rounded,

shape but most are slightly oval. Their shape, plus the fibrous covering on the outside of the tuber and their habit of being strung together, makes identifying these wild root vegetables quite easy.

Members of the pea family, groundnuts send out vines, which have pealike leaves and blossoms. The leaves are divided into five or more pointed leaflets. Each leaflet is broad at the base but gradually tapers to a sharp end. The leaves are smooth and lack teeth. The pealike blossoms come in a range of shades from almost chocolate brown to a lighter tone of burgundy.

Hikers, anglers, and others who spend time outdoors often encounter groundnut vines without realizing what they have found. The vines haven't strength enough to support themselves and so must rely on nearby vegetation. Groundnut vines grow so thickly that they easily choke out and kill other plants. Even the tenacious Japanese knotweed is no match for these aggressive vines. In my mind, any vine that can strangle Japanese knotweed to death is one mean customer.

Once you've found the vines, locating the underground tubers requires choosing one vine and tracing it down to where it leaves the ground. This is easier said than done—the vines always describe the most circuitous path possible. Upon locating the base of the vine, it's time to dig down and look for

RECIPE

Cut large groundnuts in half so they will cook through easily; leave smaller groundnuts whole. Boil in water the same as with potatoes. It's difficult to say how long it will take, since that depends upon the size and quantity of the groundnuts, but ten minutes at a rolling boil should suffice. Check for doneness with a table fork; when soft, drain and serve.

Like potatoes, boiled groundnuts go well with butter, salt, and pepper. But instead of that granular texture so common to potatoes, groundnuts more closely resemble cooked turnips. The taste, which some also liken to turnips, is sweet and mild, very satisfying.

groundnuts. In soft soil this can be as easy as pulling up the vine and mucking about barehanded in the soft loam. In other instances, digging out the tubers requires a digging tool, like a trowel.

FORAGER NOTE: Groundnuts keep in the refrigerator indefinitely, so if time constraints don't allow for immediate use, don't worry. They'll keep.

It makes sense to keep only the largest groundnuts and return smaller specimens to the ground. If the stand is of any size at all, it will harbor more groundnuts than anyone would care to deal with at one time. Don't worry about harming the stand; that would be nearly impossible. There will always be a few groundnuts left, and these can easily grow into another lush colony.

Groundnut fanciers have a brief window of opportunity in early spring when groundnuts lie exposed along riverbanks and streamsides. Here's what happens: When the ice breaks up in late winter, large blocks of jagged-edged ice are flushed downstream. On their way these floes dig up the bottom, dislodging anything in their path. Often this includes groundnuts. Once the ice melts and water drops to a normal, or seasonal, level, the forager has only to walk up and down the banks and pick up loose groundnuts.

When making a wild meal of trout and groundnuts, take a slotted vegetable peeler and remove the thin, fibrous skin. (The skin also can be removed when the product is served.) The recipe possibilities are endless, since most anything we can do with potatoes we can also do with groundnuts.

By the way, the Pilgrims had groundnuts on their table at the first Thanksgiving. Perhaps we modern foragers could relive that event by adding boiled groundnuts to the holiday menu.

RECIPE

Groundnuts are also good when sliced and fried, the same as potatoes. Because it requires frying in bacon fat or oil and can be greasy, I make this special treat on rare occasions.

OSTRICH FERN
Pteretis pensylvanica

Synonym: Fiddlehead
Use: Cooked vegetable; cold, cooked fiddleheads can be added to salads
Range: Fertile streamsides and other rich, damp ground throughout New England
Similarity to toxic species: Pasture brakes, or bracken, a smaller fern with a nearly round stipe (stem) and a three-parted triangular blade (leaf), grow along streamsides and on damp woodland ground. Young braken are skinny, lack the deep groove of an ostrich fern (although they do have a rudimentary groove), and when young are a reddish-brown color as opposed to the emerald green of the ostrich fern. Bracken fiddleheads are scrawny, with an unfinished look. Bracken are suspected of being carcinogenic when consumed in large quantities over an extended period. Also, raw or only slightly cooked bracken can cause intestinal upset.
Best time: Early spring. This may vary from northern to southern regions, but ostrich fern is usually ready mid- to late April in the south and mid-May in the north. In Aroostook County, Maine, fiddleheads persist until June.
Status: Common and abundant
Tools needed: Must be picked by hand

The emerging ostrich fern frond is called a fiddlehead. In fact, all ferns go through the fiddlehead stage. The likeness to the curled headstock of a violin, or fiddle, is striking. But from here, things become confusing. New

FORAGER NOTE: Never use raw fiddleheads in a salad; they have a profound laxative effect.

Englanders, being frugal of words, simply call immature ostrich fern fronds fiddleheads. Suffice it to say, in New England fiddlehead means "ostrich fern."

Ostrich fern, fiddlehead . . . oh, what the heck. From here on I'll simply refer to them as fiddleheads too. Fiddleheads are easy to identify. The stem has a deep groove, deeper than the slight groove on any other fern. It has a shiny, green color and is smooth as glass. The curled part, the actual fiddlehead (the folded, curled embryonic fern), is tightly packed, yet by careful unwinding it is possible to uncurl and get a look at the baby plant. Both sides of the fiddlehead are encased in a thin, brown, parchment-like material.

"Fiddleheading"—walking the streamsides in early spring in search of fiddleheads—is dear to the hearts of many New England country folk. Although most rural people have largely forsaken foraging as a way of life, many continue to go fiddleheading. And those who for physical or other reasons cannot go fiddleheading don't go without their fiddleheads. That's what friends are for—to supply fiddleheads to those who need them. Even city dwellers get in the act: Fiddleheads are a regular seasonal offering at health food stores and supermarkets. Some places even stock canned fiddleheads, right along with the canned peas and other, more common fodder. Fiddleheads are a New England staple.

Considerable mystique is attached to fiddleheads and fiddleheading.

RECIPE

Fresh, boiled fiddleheads are a springtime staple. For some the first fiddleheads must be eaten with the first mess of brook trout; the two go naturally together. But the trout are a luxury, not a necessity. The basic fiddlehead recipe is simplicity itself:

Boil water in a medium saucepan and add the fresh fiddleheads. Boil until the fiddleheads droop when picked up with a fork, and quickly remove from the water lest the fiddleheads become too soft. Serve with butter and (in this case, it is traditional) a liberal sprinkling of cider vinegar. If any fiddleheads remain, they can be cooled in the refrigerator and used either alone or with other ingredients in a salad.

The locations of prime fiddle-head patches are zealously guarded, although goodness knows why: Almost any streamside is dotted with patches of fiddleheads, and practically all the major rivers in New England, especially northern New England, have fiddleheads growing along their banks.

Fiddleheads are best picked when the stem is only an inch or two long and the heads are still tightly packed. The technique is simple: Grasp the stem as close to the ground as possible and bend until it snaps.

FORAGER NOTE: The brown, parchment-like material that clings to either side of the fiddlehead is easily removed in the woods. Some people leave it on and attempt to wash it off when they get home. Unfortunately, wetting the stuff makes it stick like glue, rendering it very difficult to remove.

Here are a few tips for the novice fiddlehead picker. First, pay close attention to the temperature. As soon as the ground has thawed and the first few black-flies (biting gnats, the bane of early-spring foragers) appear, it is time to check the fiddlehead patch. Fiddleheads, like some mushrooms, erupt practically over-night. So if the fiddleheads are not quite up yet, wait a few days and check again.

Don't neglect the hard-to-reach spots. Paw through the mats of dead grass, and pay special attention to the south side of old half-rotten logs. Sometimes the biggest and best fiddleheads are hidden in such spots.

What if someone else has already visited the fiddlehead patch? Don't despair. The root crowns produce multiple fronds over an extended period. They just keep coming. Old-time fiddleheaders insist that it weakens the plant to pick all the fiddleheads from a clump and that it is prudent to leave at least one remaining. Whether or not this helps the resource, it certainly is a nice way to view things. No matter what plant we are harvesting, we should never take it all.

It is easiest to remove the brown parchment before the fiddlehead is picked. Either pull the stuff off or tweak the fiddlehead with a forefinger. If some parchment remains after the fiddlehead is picked, tap the fiddlehead to dislodge it. Above all, remove the brown stuff before rinsing the fiddleheads. Any remaining parchment can easily be removed at home.

FREEZING

Fiddleheads are one of my wintertime staples. They keep for more than a year in the freezer, with no appreciable loss of flavor or change in texture. I place the individual bags of fiddleheads in plastic margarine tubs before freezing. Two bags easily fit in one sixteen-ounce tub. The tubs afford additional protection for the produce and stack neatly.

RECIPE

Fiddleheads can also be deep-fried, in the manner of clams or scallops. Dip the raw fiddleheads in a batter, immerse in hot oil, and drain. They're yummy.

EXTRA RECIPE

This is one of my favorite fiddlehead recipes: Boil the fiddleheads according to the standard method, and drain them thoroughly. Next line the bottom of a greased, ovenproof baking dish with a thin layer of the cooked fiddleheads. Now drizzle any kind of cheese sauce (my favorite is Alfredo) on the fiddleheads. Repeat the process by layering fiddleheads and cheese sauce until either the dish is full or the fiddleheads are used up. Finally sprinkle bread crumbs (I make my own seasoned bread crumbs with day-old bread that I save in a sealed Mason jar along with my own dried thyme, basil, and oregano) on the top layer of cheese and bake at 350°F for thirty minutes or until the top is slightly browned. The finished product is a unique, delicious main-dish meal.

STINGING NETTLE
Urtica dioica

Uses: Cooked vegetable, soup
Range: Throughout New England on fertile, rich soil, particularly along fertile streamsides
Similarity to toxic species: None
Best time: Late April through late May
Status: Common and abundant
Tools needed: Leather or thick rubber gloves

Most of us have accidentally brushed against stinging nettles. The resulting sting is as sharp and unpleasant as any bee sting. That's because nettle spines contain formic acid, the same stuff many venomous insects carry. Nettle stings, however painful, don't last long and are soon forgotten. Some people consider the occasional nettle sting to have a prophylactic effect upon the pain of arthritis. (The same is often said regarding honeybee stings.)

Nettles are an early-spring plant and can usually be found about the same time that ostrich fern fiddleheads are ready for picking, and often in the same location. A few years ago a local photographer who specializes in plants asked me to take her to one of my favorite fiddlehead locations so she could take some close-up shots for a magazine. As she was zooming in on a clump of fiddleheads, she casually asked if I knew where she might find some stinging nettles. At that very

moment my wrist brushed against a nettle plant. With gritted teeth because of the burning pain, I said, simply, "Yes." I hadn't noticed nettles along that particular section of stream before.

Nettle shoots spring from a labyrinth of buried rhizomes. Each spring the rhizomes push up a new crop of stinging nettles. Only the young shoots are eaten. Mature nettle plants are tough and full of grit.

Nettles have slender flower clusters that sprout from the leaf axils. Recognizing the flowers is little help to the forager, however, except to mark the spot for the following spring. By the time nettles flower, they are gone by—too far advanced in size for eating. It is better to learn to recognize the immature nettles by the leaves. The leaves are generally of a slender, oval shape; are sharply pointed at the tip; and have unusually long petioles, or stems. Further, the leaves grow opposite each other and have well-defined, sharp teeth. The upper and lower parts of the leaves, as well as the stem, are covered with fine, hairy bristles, from which comes the sting. Overall, the young plants (best picked when less than 12 inches tall) have a wilted, drooping appearance.

Wear good, protective gloves when picking nettles. It is best to wear long sleeves or, better yet, a sturdy denim jacket to protect wrists and arms. The young nettles are best when snapped or broken near the base of the stem. Sometimes, especially in soft, deep soil, the entire shoot will be dislodged and pull free from the ground. If that happens, don't worry. The underground rhizomes will soon send forth another shoot.

RECIPE

Boiled nettles may sound homely and plain, but no better vegetable can be found in the wild or in the supermarket. In a medium saucepan add a scant bit of water—just enough to cover the bottom. Rinse the nettles, but don't drain them. Turn on the heat, and add the nettles as soon as the water bubbles. Cover, reduce the heat to low, and simmer for fifteen or twenty minutes.

Lift the cooked nettles from the pot, allowing them to drain back into the cooking liquid. Do not discard the liquid. It will be used later as a soup. Serve the nettles with a pat of butter and salt and pepper. A more palatable, wholesome vegetable cannot be found.

The juice, which by now has turned a dark green, is the base for a unique soup. Save the soup for another time, or serve it separately with the cooked nettles. Add salt, pepper, and a splash of cider vinegar to the nettle broth. Let the mixture simmer before serving in small soup bowls. Nettle broth is surprisingly pleasant and tasty when served cold as well as hot.

Place the nettles—tender stem, leaves, and tops—in a pail, basket, or canvas bag. At home, still wearing gloves, spread the nettles on a tabletop to search for any foreign matter: sticks, grasses, and so on. The nettles then can be chopped with a knife or shears. After washing, the nettles can be cooked immediately or refrigerated for a day or so.

EXTRA RECIPE

For a more complex nettle soup, combine chicken stock or canned broth with nettle leaves, a cut-up onion, a pat of butter, and salt and pepper. Let the mixture simmer until the onion is cooked through. In Scotland a bit of heavy cream is added to the nettle soup before serving. This Scottish version is hearty, satisfying fare.

CURLED DOCK
Rumex crispus (also other *Rumex* species)

Use: Cooked vegetable
Range: Throughout New England along fertile streamsides, in rich fields, and on damp roadsides
Similarity to toxic species: None; all the dock varieties are edible.
Best time: Late April through early June
Status: Common and abundant; a hardy weed
Tools needed: None

During the dark days of the Great Depression, my family enjoyed an eclectic diet, eating such things as roasted young woodchuck, smoked white suckers, sucker roe, and curled dock. Later, because these things reminded them of the hard times, they avoided them. It wasn't until late in his life that my grandpa told me about dock. "It's like spinach," he said, without much enthusiasm. It happened that this was in early May, when the dock was at its peak. I went out that afternoon, picked a bunch of tender young dock leaves, brought them home, and steamed them. They did taste something like spinach but had a better flavor.

Many years after my initial experience with dock, I went on a weeklong camping and fishing trip in northern Maine. Vowing to live off the land for a week, I brought no food except salt, pepper, and butter. The trout cooperated, providing the meat part of my diet. Then there was the dock. The big, mixed-growth northern forest is perhaps the most difficult place for a forager to find sufficient provender. Since this was June, even the cutover areas offered but scant fare; the raspberries were not quite ripe, and the blueberries were still at the tiny, hard green stage. Had it not been for the ubiquitous dock, my trip would probably have been cut short. By the week's end, it became difficult to swallow another forkful of trout, but I still enjoyed the dock.

Dock, a member of the buckwheat family, is often said to be a bitter herb, fit to eat only after being boiled in three changes of water. This may be true in late summer, when the curly leaves become tough and unpalatable. But in season, which can be as early as April in southern New England and as late as early June in northern Maine, dock is a superior vegetable, sweet and mild.

When growing in the open, dock can attain heights of up to 4 feet, but most plants are between 1 and 2 feet tall. The individual leaves—the edible part of the plant—are thin and up to 10 inches long; they have wavy edges, hence the name curled dock. A papery, moist membrane surrounds the petiole, or leafstalk, where it attaches to the stem. The seed stalk is covered with winged, chestnut-brown seeds in fall. These are popular in dried flower arrangements. It is possible to dry these seeds, thresh them, and grind them into a flour substitute, but the effort involved is (for me, at least) too great in comparison to the end result.

Broad-leaved, or red-veined, dock has wide, heart-shaped leaves. This dock is best gathered in early spring because it becomes bitter later in summer. Broad-leaved dock often grows in the beds of seasonal streams and is one of the earliest greens to be found in spring, often presenting itself when patches of snow still cling to the north-facing slopes.

RECIPE

Cook dock as you would spinach. Place the fresh leaves in boiling water and cook until tender. Dock retains most of its bulk in cooking, with the cooked product occupying about as much space as the raw material. Drain immediately after cooking; season with butter, salt, and pepper. Dock is enhanced by a splash of cider vinegar, but this isn't necessary.

Besides tasting as good or better than any similar cultivated leafy vegetable, dock is a veritable powerhouse of vitamins, particularly vitamins A and C. Dock is also a significant source of protein. Want to go on a health food regimen? Incorporate dock into your diet. Fresh trout helps too.

Remedy: *Folklore about dock is mostly concerned with its curative powers for stinging nettle rash. Country children seem to know intuitively to rub crushed dock leaves on nettle stings. Even children whose parents know nothing about dock or nettles use dock. My guess is that ongoing generations of children hand this knowledge down without the slightest need of adult intercession.*

WILD OATS
Uvularia sessilifolia

Synonym: Sessile bellwort
Uses: Cooked vegetable, salad ingredient, trail nibble
Range: Throughout New England along streamsides and in damp, rich woodlands
Similarity to toxic species: None
Best time: April and May
Status: Locally abundant
Tools needed: None

One particular day along Maine's Kennebec River stands out in my mind for two reasons: First, red quill mayflies hatched in profuse quantities, and huge brown trout noisily slurped them in. Second, the fertile plain along the river was covered with ostrich fern fiddleheads, mingled with dense patches of wild oats. All these pleasing items in one place, at one time, made a big impression on me.

FORAGER NOTE: Add a handful of wild oats shoots to your gathering basket, especially if enough other plants are around that can be combined to make a wild salad. Oat shoots will make a pleasant addition.

Wild oats, actually a member of the lily family, sometimes reach a foot in height but more often are a little more than half that. The forked stems remind me of thin, little chicken wishbones. The leaves are sessile, attached directly to the stem. When in bloom, the bell-shaped (hence the other common name, bellwort) yellow flowers hang from a thin stem.

Despite my inclination for eating wild oats raw, the cooked vegetable is fine table fare too. If lots of wild oats are present on your local fertile streamside, by all means go for it. These branched perennial plants are a real symbol of the New England spring in all its finery, and they are there for us to enjoy.

Trail food: *My favorite way to enjoy wild oats is to pick the young shoot, strip away all green matter, and nibble them raw. One or two shoots are enough to assuage my appetite until more substantial fare can be found.*

MARSH MARIGOLD
Caltha palustris

Synonym: Cowslip
Use: Cooked vegetable
Range: Throughout New England along slow-moving streams and in swamps
Similarity to toxic species: The flowers are somewhat similar to those of the toxic common buttercup. The leaves of the two species are markedly different, however.
Best time: May
Status: Locally abundant
Tools needed: A jackknife helps when cutting individual leaves.

Except that marsh marigolds do grow in marshes, both common names for this pretty, springtime plant are misleading. Marsh marigold is not a marigold and is definitely not a cowslip, but instead is closely related to the common buttercup. This highlights the value of using the scientific name of our favorite plants whenever possible instead of the often-misleading common name.

One particular stand of marsh marigolds is impressed upon my memory as surely as if it were in a color photograph. These marsh marigolds grow in the middle of a little winding stream in the headwaters of a great wetland. When the sun strikes the bright yellow flowers, they shine like beacons.

Marsh marigolds were another one of my grandparents' Great Depression staples and therefore were not on the table when I came along. They told me about the plants, though, with some degree of fondness.

Marsh marigolds stand from 6 inches to 2 feet tall. The bright yellow flowers resemble common buttercup flowers. The dark green leaves, which are the parts that are eaten, are shiny and heart or kidney shaped. The stem is hollow. The flowers close at night and open during the day.

The time to harvest marsh marigold leaves is before and during the time the plant is in blossom. Carefully cut or snap the leaves from the stalk. This will not harm the plant if only a few leaves are taken.

Most people cook marsh marigold leaves in two or three changes of water in order to make the taste milder. The leaves contain a sharp-tasting toxin that is rendered harmless by boiling, and the different cooking waters also remove any trace of the toxin. I cook the leaves in only one water without detecting a strong taste or suffering any ill effects.

Marsh marigold leaves are prime when ostrich fern fiddleheads, dock, stinging nettles, and wild oats are ready. It's not unusual for all these plants to be found in the same location.

> FORAGER NOTE: Springtime in New England means bugs—both mosquitoes and, in the northern climes, blackflies. Insect repellent containing DEET will keep the bugs from biting. Make sure to get the bug dope on your wrists, the back of your neck, and around pant cuffs and sock tops. Wash the repellent off at the end of the day. Some people are afraid of the chemicals in bug repellents and wear a head net instead. Head nets drive me to distraction, though, because they are so hard to see through.

RECIPE

No matter how many changes of water you use, get the water boiling first. Thoroughly wash the leaves, and then immerse them in the boiling water. Leave the leaves in the boiling water for at least twenty minutes, drain the leaves, and discard the water. Season to taste; I add butter, salt, and pepper.

Plants of Disturbed and Cultivated Ground

The next time the highway department grades a nearby roadside ditch, take note. That now-barren ground will in a short time be covered with a variety of interesting, and useful, wild plants. Seeds, brought in on the wind, deposited by birds, or perhaps already present in the ground, dormant and waiting for the grader blade to stir them to life, will germinate, and a rush of growth will magically transform the formerly lifeless roadside into a carpet of green.

Then there is the cultivated ground—perhaps our own flower or vegetable gardens or the local farmer's cornfield—where "weeds" vex and thwart all but the most determined efforts to eradicate them. Actually, many of the plants that people strive to conquer are nutritionally superior to the cultivated plants that displace them.

Nature will not permit disturbed and cultivated ground to remain barren for long. And ironically the act of cultivating, grading, or scraping is what makes this ground suitable for so many useful plants. Our efforts to make letter-perfect garden beds only encourage the invading weeds. Perhaps it's time we foragers recognize that wild plants have a right to grow alongside our cabbage and tomatoes and consider the vegetable plot a multiuse area, home to both cultivated plants and their valuable wild cousins.

LAMB'S-QUARTERS
Chenopodium album

Synonym: Pigweed
Uses: Cooked vegetable, attractor plant for leaf miners
Range: Cultivated and recently disturbed ground throughout New England
Similarity to toxic species: Mexican tea (*C. ambrosioides*) is a smelly look-alike. The difference is easily determined—the Mexican tea leaves smell like varnish.
Best time: May and throughout the growing season
Status: Common; despised as a difficult-to-eradicate weed
Tools needed: None

Lamb's-quarters, another member of the goosefoot family, are easily identified. Mature plants can grow to a height of 3 feet. The spear-shaped leaves have wide, uneven teeth and are covered with a grainy white substance. If in doubt, rub the leaf with a finger; the white powder will feel rough and coarse. In late summer tiny black seeds by the thousands are formed on the flower stem, which grows in the leaf axils.

By the time the grass needs the first mowing of the season, it is time to thin the lamb's-quarters in my vegetable garden. This is an eagerly anticipated event on my gardening calendar. The diminutive lamb's-quarters grow overly thick and must be thinned. At the same time, the 3- to 5-inch plants provide the season's first meal of lamb's-quarters.

The best areas of the garden to encourage lamb's-quarters are where late-season crops such as winter squash are planted. These tender plants cannot stand much cold, and seeds or seedlings fail if planted while the soil temperature is much less than seventy degrees. The result is that these particular garden beds are vacant in spring, while other beds are active. Instead of planting quick-growing spring crops like radishes or lettuce, I allow the lamb's-quarters to do their thing, thinning the crop as needed for the table.

Here's a practical tip for thinning lamb's-quarters and similar vegetables: Don't pull the plant up by the roots. This creates extra work because the roots have to be removed later, a tedious task. Better to use kitchen shears and snip the tender plants near the ground. This makes cleaning the harvest easier; at the same time, the intact roots help improve the tilth, or friability, of the soil.

When the lamb's-quarters are about a foot high, the time is right to harvest a great quantity. Most of the plant, except for the thickest part of the stem, can be taken.

About those lamb's-quarters plants in the winter squash bed: Rather than harvest all the plants, I leave one or two of the biggest, lushest specimens to grow to maturity. This kills two birds with one proverbial stone. First, it guarantees a crop of lamb's-quarters seeds and an ongoing supply of lamb's-quarters. Second, the fully grown plants act as an attractor for leaf miners, those maddening little pests that leave ugly "snail trails" on the leaves of cultivated plants as they burrow through the leaf. Leaf miners love to work their way through lamb's-quarters leaves—the bigger and thicker the lamb's-quarters plant, the better the cursed bugs like them. I'm convinced that leaf miner damage to my cultivated crops is lessened considerably because of the presence of the lamb's-quarters.

But that's not all. After the leaf miners have had their fling, the lamb's-quarters continue to sprout new branchlets and leaves. It helps to do some light pruning throughout the season to encourage new growth. By fall, just before the big killing frosts reduce all tender vegetation to blackened, withered crisps, the last picking of lamb's-quarters can take place.

RECIPE

You can either steam or boil lamb's-quarters, just as you would orache. Drop lamb's-quarters in boiling water and cook only until the plants turn dark green. This takes only about two minutes. Drain immediately to stop further cooking.

From the lengths I go to for lamb's-quarters, you've doubtless guessed that I think the plants are worth the effort. But what about those who don't have garden beds or a place to encourage lamb's-quarters? Don't despair.

Go to a spot where the ground was disturbed the previous year, perhaps a vacant lot or some such place. Lamb's-quarters are efficient pioneers and are able to take advantage of ripe ground at a moment's notice. For those living in the country, head to the nearest farm and ask the farmer for permission to pick some "weeds" from the edge of his manure pile. Lamb's-quarters don't like fresh manure but thrive on the ancient rotted stuff, such as is found behind and around the edges of manure piles.

It wouldn't be fitting to end this entry with talk of foraging around old manure piles. Lamb's-quarters are a noble plant and deserve better. If this plant ever achieves the recognition that is its due, lamb's-quarters will be sold in supermarkets and health food stores at outrageous prices. People will scour the countryside looking for stands of lamb's-quarters. But until that happens, we foragers have unlimited access to one of the tastiest and most nutritious plants in the world—for free. Perhaps we should keep it our secret for just a little longer.

FREEZING

Lamb's-quarters blanch quickly. Immerse in boiling water until leaves wilt and turn dark green. After blanching, chill in ice-cold water, drain, put into pint freezer bags, and lovingly place them in the freezer. Lamb's-quarters last up to a year in the freezer without any discernible change in taste or texture.

DAME'S ROCKET
Hesperis matronalis

Synonyms: Wild phlox, dame's violet
Use: Cooked vegetable
Range: Throughout New England
Similarity to toxic species: None
Best time: May and again in October and November
Status: Locally abundant
Tools needed: None

Like so many of our beloved wild plants, dame's rocket is nonnative. It probably came here by seed, perhaps mixed in with hay for livestock. Or perhaps, since it was once a cultivated garden flower, it was brought across the sea with an eye to establishing a colony in the New World. However it got here, it is widespread and usually occurs in large colonies.

Although I was aware that these plants belonged to the mustard family and as such were probably edible, for years I was reluctant to destroy my beautiful, sweet-smelling flowers by eating them.

When I eventually grew enough dame's rocket that sacrificing a few plants for the table wasn't a big deal, I clipped a handful of leaves and gently boiled them in a slight amount of water. The taste, reminiscent of spinach and also horseradish, was mild and, I thought, very sweet.

Pick the leaves in spring, before the plant sends up its seed stalk. Once that happens, the leaves become too strong-tasting to be palatable. Rinse and drain the leaves, and set a slight amount of water to boiling in a saucepan. Cook the leaves for only a few minutes, until they turn a deeper shade of green and wilt when picked up with a fork.

A bowl of freshly cooked dame's rocket leaves calls for butter and a dash of cider vinegar. Season to taste.

Dame's rocket quite closely resembles garden phlox. Garden phlox runs 2 to 6 feet tall, has same-color flowers as dame's rocket, and has lance-shaped leaves. But there the similarity ends. True phlox has five-petaled flowers; dame's rocket, being a mustard, has only four petals. Also, the lance-shaped leaves of dame's rocket are quite coarsely toothed, while phlox leaves are smooth-edged.

One nineteenth-century handbook on plants goes into great detail on how best to propagate dame's rocket, clear evidence of the great esteem gardeners once held for the plant. Since that time dame's rocket has spread on its own and now grows in cultivated ground and along garden edges, on railroad rights-of-way, and even on rich streamsides. The plant self-seeds readily, which explains its wide distribution.

My experience with dame's rocket dates back to a walk down a path to a local river one June. I passed through a large colony of blooming rocket, and the powerful fragrance enticed me to linger and breathe it in. Later that summer I passed by the same colony of dame's rocket. By then the plant had produced long, mustard-like seedpods. I filled my pockets with the not-quite-ripe seedpods and upon returning home placed them on a shelf to dry. When the tiny seeds were fully dried, I sprinkled them around the edge of my lawn and even on cultivated ground where some culinary herbs grew.

In time I had several large clumps of dame's rocket, and these white, pink, and purple flowers were so fragrant that I spent many evenings outside, just walking about delighting in their sweet aroma. Rocket becomes far more fragrant in the evening, thus the first half of its botanical name, *Hesperis,* which comes from *Hesperos,* the evening star.

Dame's rocket grows from a basal rosette, or a whorl or round clump of leaves emerging from a central base. The young leaves are at their best in May and even early June, at least in northern Maine.

Later in fall, after the aerial stem dies back, only the basal rosette of leaves remain. These are still edible, but I find them not quite as mild as in spring. In fact, nibbling a raw leaf in late November, I was reminded of sea-rocket (*Cakile edentula*). This isn't surprising, since both plants belong to the mustard family. Sea-rocket has a strong mustard flavor, very spicy.

🍃🌿 Trail food: *Dame's rocket flowers and buds are edible too and are best eaten out of hand as a trail nibble. I still have a hard time removing a bud from one of my resident plants, knowing that if left alone, it will soon become a colorful, fragrant flower. All the same, when dame's rocket presents itself during any of my trips afield, I'm more than willing to nibble.*

RECIPE

Dame's rocket flowers make an attractive addition to a simple salad. Just sprinkle a handful of the flowers on top, as a last touch. Dame's rocket proves that we can have our flowers and eat them too.

COMMON SORREL
Rumex acetosella

Synonyms: Sheep sorrel, sour grass, sour dock
Uses: Trail nibble, salad or sandwich ingredient, potherb
Range: Throughout New England
Similarity to toxic species: None
Best time: May through August
Status: Abundant and underutilized; considered a weed
Tools needed: None

Imagine a typical cast of characters in a Shakespeare play. Among these expect to find "attendants (with halberds)." Indeed, the leaves of common sorrel bear

RECIPE

Common sorrel's trademark sour taste makes it more than just a satisfying thirst quencher. The tender leaves make a fine addition to any sandwich, taking the place of pickles.

a striking resemblance to the long, pointed, deeply barbed weapon employed by guards and other military characters of old. Another synonym would be "arrowhead shaped."

The fact that common sorrel is edible may for the most part be lost on adults, but children seem to have an instinctive knowledge of its use. I don't recall an adult ever telling me that sorrel was edible, yet I unques-

FORAGER NOTE: The first half of common sorrel's scientific name, *Rumex*, dates back to the *rumo* of Roman times. It means "to suck" and alludes to the ancient practice of sucking on the leaves in order to allay thirst.

tioningly nibbled it at every opportunity. Somewhere along the road to adulthood, this instinctive familiarity with edible wild plants disappears, at least for most people.

Common sorrel appears anywhere and everywhere, provided it has ample sunlight. From fields and forest openings to lawns, gravel banks, roadsides, and even flower and vegetable gardens, common sorrel grows and thrives.

Beginning in spring, when garden weeds first begin to put on growth for the new season, look for small, low-growing clumps of common sorrel. Locate them by their distinctive leaves. Later in the season the clump sends up a flower spike, intermittently covered in tiny, reddish flowers.

Common sorrel contains oxalic acid, but so do many cultivated garden vegetables, including parsley, garlic, radishes, spinach, and lettuce. In order to suffer any ill effects from the oxalic acid in sorrel, a person would need to consume a massive amount raw daily for an extended period of time. Cooked sorrel poses even less of a threat, since boiling considerably reduces the oxalic acid content.

All this simply points out that too much of any one thing might not be a good thing. Fortunately for wild-food foragers, the great wealth of different plant species available at any particular time precludes overindulgence in any one plant.

Common sorrel definitely has its place on the list of the forager's seasonal treats.

RECIPE

Salads also benefit from the addition of sorrel leaves. It might be best to chop the leaves first; a slaw cutter works handily for this job. A kitchen knife, such as one used to chop onions and other vegetables, can serve the same purpose.

Trail food: *For me, the best use of common sorrel is to pick the young leaves and nibble away. Such a simple way to enjoy nature's bounty—no lengthy preparation, no complicated recipes, no drying or further processing necessary. Just pick and enjoy. That is how I've used sorrel from the very beginning, and I still like to go out to my garden and eat two or three leaves.*

RECIPE

Some people use sorrel as a potherb, or cooked green. If preparing sorrel this way, just remember two things: First, don't overcook; treat sorrel like spinach. Keep watch on it while boiling, and when it becomes limp, drain and serve. Second, remember that sorrel loses bulk in cooking; collect perhaps twice the amount that would seem ample for a normal serving.

QUICKWEED
Galinsoga ciliata (also *G. parviflora* where available)

Synonym: Galinsoga
Use: Cooked vegetable
Range: Throughout New England
Similarity to toxic species: None
Best time: July through September
Status: Widely abundant; a despised weed
Tools needed: None

Quickweed, a member of the daisy family, grows on recently disturbed ground. Quickweed is not an old-time favorite of New England foragers, nor does it have much of a history in the region. It is a relatively new plant, having crept in from the Deep South and Mexico, and many otherwise knowledgeable foragers have yet to discover it.

My first encounter with quickweed came as a result of a load of composted cow manure being delivered to my garden. The stuff was laden with quickweed, which immediately took over several of my garden beds. At first I ruthlessly pulled each plant (an easy job—it's shallow rooted) from the garden, hoping to get rid of this strange invader once and for all. Failing that, I determined to learn more about this noxious intruder. My sleuthing paid off when I discovered that

Pick a good mess of quickweed for the first try—it loses some bulk in cooking. My favorite way is to boil it for about ten minutes, drain, and serve with butter and a bit of salt. Vinegar complements quickweed, but that is a matter of taste. For me, the plant doesn't need any added flavor.

quickweed is edible. I allowed the tiny plants that remained to grow to usable size, picked them, boiled them for a little less than ten minutes, and sat at the table for my first taste of quickweed. The stuff I had worked so hard to eradicate was better in all respects than most of my cultivated vegetables.

Quickweed is identified by its ovate, roughly toothed leaves, hairy stem (at least with *G. ciliata*), and unfinished-looking flower. The flower resembles a miniature daisy with half the petals removed at equal intervals, leaving a tiny yellow disc and four tiny groups of petals at the four compass points.

This inconspicuous, lowly invader from the warmer climes may be hated by most people, but those of us who know its virtues praise it.

FIELD PEPPERGRASS
Lepidium campestre

Synonym: Cow cress
Uses: Trail nibble, salad ingredient, cooked vegetable
Range: Throughout New England
Similarity to toxic species: None
Best time: May and June; new growth continues all summer and into fall, especially after the first frost.
Status: Common and abundant; an alien weed despised by most
Tools needed: None

Like so many of my favorite wild vegetables, peppergrass came to my garden via a truckload of composted cow manure. The compost had lain uncovered for some time before being sold, and seeds of various "weeds" had sufficient time to take hold. The four petals on the little yellow flowers told me immediately that here was one of the mustards. Now instead of having to drive hither and yon to get the occasional supply of peppergrass, my own personal supply was solidly established. The farmer didn't realize the good deal he had given me.

Another member of the *Lepidium* genus, poor-man's-pepper (*L. virginicum,* which has stalked leaves), is equally as good as field peppergrass, and the two can be used interchangeably. And speaking of related plants, the young leaves of common horseradish (*Armoracia lapathifolia*) can be used the same as peppergrass. This was news to me when, a few years ago, an old-timer asked my opinion of boiled horseradish leaves. Having never tried them, I had no opinion. That changed after my first taste of the spicy greens. They added much-appreciated zest to my noontime meal.

Learn to recognize field peppergrass by its dark green, slender, deeply toothed leaves, which are attached directly to the stem of the plant, and by the thin flower spikes with their small, four-petaled white flowers. Once this tentative identification is made, it is safe to take a small nibble. The pungent mustard flavor, while not strong or offensive, is immediately evident.

Trail food: *As with so many other wild plants, my all-time favorite use of field peppergrass is as a casual nibble. When passing field peppergrass, I tend to pick a few tender tips and leaves and chew on them without giving the act much thought.*

GREEN AMARANTH
Amaranthus retroflexus

Synonyms: Amaranth, pigweed
Use: Cooked vegetable
Range: Throughout New England
Similarity to toxic species: None
Best time: From the time it is big enough to pick, usually May, until the plant is killed by frost
Status: Common and abundant; uncontrollable weed
Tools needed: None

Amaranth is an aggressive transplant from the South and is believed to have been among the earliest plants cultivated by North American Indians. It does best on cultivated ground; commercial fields that are plowed and harrowed each year are a favorite location. One place stands out in my mind—a massive cornfield filled with silage corn for use as dairy cow feed. The corn was harvested and chopped, leaving a field half filled with 2-foot-tall amaranth plants. The leaves from the amaranth in this field could have fed all the inhabitants of the town for a month, three times daily, but the farmer plowed this valuable green vegetable back into the ground, along with the corn stubble. This scenario is reenacted each year across the United States and southern Canada.

Green amaranth is easy to identify. The leaves are the most important feature. They have blunt ends, are wider at the base than at the tip, and have a prominent center rib, with alternate veins issuing from the midrib. They are dark green on top but have a gauzy, reddish hue on the bottom. The seed spikes, which appear in late summer, are somewhat prickly.

Amaranth makes a palatable, albeit somewhat mild, spinach substitute. Once I diligently tended my spinach crop. In order to give the spinach every opportunity, I pulled out all the amaranth, the primary weed in the spinach bed. Even so, the spinach was slow growing, and when it finally achieved a useful size, it bolted. After the spinach was long gone, amaranth continued to grow. I ate it all season long, and it was as good as the spinach I had wasted so much time on.

Eventually I realized that it was impractical to raise spinach when amaranth was so abundant. I don't grow spinach anymore.

FREEZING

Amaranth keeps well in the freezer. Blanch amaranth in boiling water for one minute and then place in a pan of cold water to cool. Drain and place in plastic freezer bags and put these in the freezer.

PURSLANE
Portulaca oleracea

Synonym: Pusley
Uses: Cooked vegetable, salad ingredient
Range: Throughout New England, in cultivated soil
Similarity to toxic species: None
Best time: June through September
Status: Abundant weed
Tools needed: None

It has taken me a lifetime to say "purslane" instead of "pusley," the latter being the old-time name that my grandpa used for this ubiquitous vining plant. Purslane is universally despised by gardeners, because once it appears it cannot be

RECIPE

Cleaned, chopped purslane can be boiled or steamed for about ten minutes, drained, and served as a green vegetable with the usual butter, salt, and pepper.

My favorite use of purslane is in stir-fries. It can be the sole ingredient or one of many in a delightful wild stir-fry.

For the first purslane stir-fry of the season, don't add other ingredients; instead, fully appreciate this tender, sweet vegetable alone. Use a good, low-sodium soy sauce and make your own hot mustard by mixing powdered English mustard with water and perhaps a drop of white vinegar. Stir-fry the purslane until it is limp, and serve with a side dish of rice—a cheap meal, but one as nutritious and savory as all get out.

eradicated. But I'm glad purslane found its way to my vegetable garden. Now I don't have to rely on others for my supply of this prized vegetable.

Before purslane invaded my vegetable garden, I decided to try raising the cultivated variety, something called golden purslane. The golden purslane didn't stack up to its wild cousin. The germination rate was poor; the stuff didn't have the sprawling habit of wild purslane either and thus didn't offer a sufficient quantity for a big purslane eater like me. And insects attacked it with a vengeance, something that rarely happens to wild purslane. This was my second attempt to grow a cultivated type of a wild plant, and like the first attempt, it was a failure. It's so hard to improve on something that is pretty near perfect in the first place.

Purslane is readily identified by its dark green, paddle-shaped leaves, each approximate ½ to ¾ inch long. These leaves are not green on the bottom, however. Instead they have a whitish sheen that sparkles in the sun, something like moonlight reflecting off freshly fallen snow. Purslane has insignificant yellow five-petaled flowers.

Rarely does purslane rise more than 1 inch above the ground. Instead the thick, reddish, succulent stem branches and spreads, like different divisions of an invading host making simultaneous flank, rear, and frontal attacks on an unsuspecting enemy.

Purslane stems can be snipped indiscriminately; new growth will soon follow. Take the ends of the stems, the most tender part. I use a colander instead of a basket for gathering. That way it is easy to take the purslane inside and rinse. Rinse thoroughly, because the stems can pick up grit from the soil. After the vegetable is thoroughly clean, chop it into 1-inch-long sections. There's no need to strip the leaves.

Purslane keeps for a long time in the crisper drawer of the refrigerator. If it gets a bit limp, soak it in cold water for five minutes, drain, and it is ready to use.

🌿 Remedy: *To paraphrase an old saw, "Purslane not only tastes good, it's good for you." Highly esteemed around the world, purslane has medicinal as well as culinary uses. First, the sticky juice from the crushed stems and leaves can be used in much the same way aloe juice is used for relief from stings, burns, and bites. The cooked vegetable is rich in vitamins C and A, as well as the beneficial omega-3 acids. Purslane also contains good amounts of calcium and phosphorus. It's a regular natural vitamin pill.*

LADY'S THUMB
Polygonum persicaria

Synonym: Redleg
Use: Cooked vegetable
Range: In waste places throughout New England, particularly damp areas
Similarity to toxic species: None
Best time: May through September
Status: Widespread and common
Tools needed: None

Lady's thumb, another member of the widespread buckwheat family, is one of those plants that everybody sees but few take time to identify. For years I didn't know what it was, referring to it in my mind as "that droopy-looking weed that grows across the street by the henhouse." But when it appeared near my place, I decided it was time to learn more about it. The lady's thumb turned out to be a delicious boiling green, which came as no surprise considering its relationship to another eminently edible plant, Japanese knotweed. To my knowledge, lady's thumb has never been and is not currently a popular wild food in New England. I'm the only person I know who eats it—and maybe now you.

Lady's thumb has several identifying features. The dark blotch on the upper part of each leaf is its trademark, the so-called lady's thumbprint. The leaves are lance shaped, with no discernible teeth. The leaf margins, however, are quite wavy. Where the leaves join the stem, they are covered by a membranous sheath, similar to the sheath on the joints of Japanese knotweed. The tiny pinkish-white flowers are borne on short spikes. Finally the plant has an overall wilted appearance, as if the hot, noonday sun was too much for it.

Lady's thumb is said to acquire a bit of an acrid taste in summer. I've never noticed this. The lady's thumb on my land seems as sweet and mild as the most tender young spinach. But since it is one of the smartweeds, and the word *smartweed* presumably refers to a peppery quality when eaten, it is possible that lady's thumb differs from place to place, which is not at all unusual.

My main problem with lady's thumb is there is not enough of it around my place to give me more than a few meals each summer. And although it would be easy enough for me to go elsewhere and gather an abundant supply, I am content to husband the local crop and appreciate what it gives me. Some things are enhanced in value if they are dear. Lady's thumb is like that.

Woodland Plants of the Mottled Shade

Old-growth forests, the kind with a dense canopy, offer little in the way of wild foods. That's also true of plantations of red pine and of the fir "jungles" of northern New England. They're simply not likely places for the forager. That's because the plants that we seek need some measure of sun, and sun cannot penetrate a thick forest canopy.

Some of the edible wildlings, though, cannot live in direct sun either. They require mottled or dappled shade—a mixture of sun and shade. For the most part these plants live in the rich loam in or along the edges of mixed-growth woodlands. Some of the best-tasting and most interesting plants live in the mottled shade of our New England woodlands.

CLINTONIA
Clintonia borealis

Synonyms: Corn lily, blue-bead lily
Uses: Trail nibble, salad ingredient, cooked vegetable
Range: Woodland edges and rich loam throughout New England
Similarity to toxic species: At a certain point in its development, clintonia vaguely resembles lily-of-the-valley. If the broken leaf does not smell like cucumbers, avoid the plant.
Best time: May
Status: Common locally
Tools needed: A jackknife or kitchen shears help trim the young leaves.

Clintonia's appearance belies its taste. Who would think that this pretty spring wildflower, with its shiny green leaves, would taste exactly like a cucumber? This cucumber taste is convenient for people like me who hate to buy anything they can easily grow themselves—in this case, cucumbers. When cukes are not in season, the craving for them intensifies, and clintonia fills the void. While clintonia lacks any resemblance to a cucumber in texture or appearance, the fresh, chopped leaf adds an unmistakable cucumber taste to any salad. The leaves can also be boiled or steamed.

As with so many wild vegetables, clintonia must be gathered at or before one particular stage of its development, in this case before the leaves completely unfurl. Past this stage the pleasant cucumber flavor becomes rank and overpowering. Clintonia is the Jekyll and Hyde of the plant world, with both a delightful and an unpleasant side.

Here is a comparison that will help identify the young clintonia leaves: They look for all the world like starched green napkins, neatly wrapped and standing at stiff attention at the dinner table. The warmer days of June will cause the leaves to unfurl and assume a totally different appearance. The adult plant has basal leaves that are about 6 inches long, are shiny and smooth, and have a prominent midvein. The nodding yellow flowers are delicate and are borne atop a naked stalk. In midsummer the fruit, or berries, are dark blue.

Clintonia is usable for only a few short weeks out of the year. This ephemeral quality adds to the allure of this attractive and good-tasting woodland lily.

INDIAN CUCUMBER
Medeola virginiana

Use: Trail nibble
Range: Shaded woods throughout New England
Similarity to toxic species: None
Best time: June through August
Status: Locally abundant but scarce in some areas. Dig roots only from large colonies.
Tools needed: Can be extracted by hand, but a long, narrow hand trowel is helpful

Common plant names are, more often than not, misleading and confusing. Here we have a woodland plant, Indian cucumber, that tastes not the least bit like a cucumber and another woodland plant, clintonia, or corn lily, that tastes exactly like a cucumber, but is named for corn, which it definitely does not taste like. It's a conundrum.

Indian cucumber is, without question, the best raw wild edible going. The taste is sweet, mild, and a little nutty. The crisp texture of an Indian cucumber reminds me of an icicle radish. Because of its long season, availability, wide range, and exquisite flavor, Indian cucumber is a favorite of hikers and backpackers. Here is a plant that lots of people know about and everybody loves.

Notice that Indian cucumber is listed solely as a trail nibble. The roots can be pickled, but to pick that many seems greedy to me. It is better to regard Indian cucumber simply as a trail snack—a special treat when encountered by chance. Digging kills the plant, although any roots left in the ground will grow another plant. Appreciate the root of this delicious plant for what it is: a wonderfully pleasant gift of nature.

The digging may be done with a trowel, but it must not be done carelessly. That's because the root lies horizontally in the ground, not vertically; in other words, it is at right angles to the stem. Because of this, it is impossible to know, without probing with the fingers, which direction the root points. Gently probe the soil at the base of the stem first, then grab the large end of the root and, while applying gentle, steady pressure, slowly work it back and forth until it breaks free. This may be likened to picking up night crawlers, those big earthworms that come out on wet nights. The worm will break if pulled roughly and quickly, but if steady, even pressure is applied, the worm soon relinquishes its grip on the sides of its burrow and can be pulled free easily. This same technique is useful in pulling carrots and parsnips. Easy does it is the key.

Indian cucumber has a singular appearance, with anywhere from five to seven or more basal leaves arranged in a whorl and a group of three to five smaller leaves atop a long, thin stem. The basal leaves are relatively slender and pointed; the leaves atop the stem are a bit fatter, resembling the leaves of another woodland plant, the bunchberry. The drooping yellow flowers are insignificant and later develop into inedible blue berries.

The stem, which can grow nearly 3 feet long, is covered with white fuzz that can be twisted between the fingers like lint or gathered in a bunch and slid up or down the stem. The roots, or rhizomes, are about 2 inches long when mature, wide at the stem end and thinly tapered at the extreme end. They have small, hairlike rootlets here and there. These rootlets ought to be rubbed off before eating.

🍃🌿 Trail food: *You might wonder how a hiker or forager could dare eat any root raw, straight from the ground. Is it sanitary? Although I usually just dig the root, wipe off all loose soil, and eat the thing as is, for safety's sake it's probably best to wash your Indian cucumber roots before eating them.*

LARGE-LEAFED ASTER
Aster macrophyllus

Use: Cooked vegetable
Range: Throughout New England
Similarity to toxic species: None
Best time: May
Status: Common and abundant, in dense colonies
Tools needed: None

Sometime in May, depending on what part of New England you're in, the large-leafed asters are ready for picking. A good rule of thumb is to seek the asters when the woodpeckers drum. Part of a woodpecker courtship ritual (various types of woodpeckers engage in this same ritual, by the way) is for the male to drum on some object that resonates loudly—usually a dead tree, but metal trash cans, aluminum boats, and even the sides of buildings are sometimes used. When the drumming becomes a regular din, when the woodlands echo with the hammering of multiple woodpeckers, all vying with one another to see who can make the most racket, that's when the large-leafed asters are prime.

A member of the daisy family, large-leafed asters lead a sort of double life. In spring the roughly toothed basal leaves are the only noticeable part of the plant.

In late summer the plant sends up a stalk and sets flowers. The flowers range from white to reddish blue. The stalk has some small, sessile leaves. Someone seeing a group of these plants in spring may have difficulty recognizing them in fall; they look so strikingly different.

It helps to recognize large-leafed asters—indeed, any edible plant—at all stages of its development. That way the plant can be noted at any time of year and visited at the correct stage for picking.

To my knowledge, large-leafed asters have absolutely no history as table fare in New England, and it is doubtful that more than a handful of people are aware of their potential as an excellent spring green. But their lack of popularity does not diminish their great taste. They are sweet and mild, with no unpleasant aftertaste.

My cottage is located in a woodland setting. The edge of my lawn is the edge of the woods and is full of large-leafed asters. All I need to do is go out with basket in hand and pick a bunch of leaves. This can be done while other components of the meal are cooking, because the leaves cook quickly. When the plants are prime, when they are no more than 4 inches long, they are a regular springtime addition to my table. Later the leaves become tough and not worth bothering with.

Don't worry about hurting the resource by picking the springtime leaves of large-leafed aster. As long as soil and light conditions are propitious, the plants will thrive. These asters are tough and durable. I once mowed a path through a big bed of large-leafed asters. They quickly grew back, and when mowed a second time, they grew back with renewed vigor. This is a hardy plant.

As with so many of these woodland plants, the season is short, so enjoy the large-leafed asters when they are ripe for the picking. They are more than worth the effort.

RECIPE

The leaves reduce slightly in bulk when boiled. Bring a little water to boiling in a pot, and drop in a few handfuls of washed large-leafed aster leaves. Cook until the leaves turn color and become limp. Drain and serve with the usual accompaniments—butter, salt, and pepper.

BUNCHBERRY
Cornus canadensis

Synonym: Dwarf cornel
Use: Trail nibble
Range: Open woodlands throughout New England
Similarity to toxic species: Many plants have red berries that should not be eaten. Exercise caution in identification.
Best time: Late June through September
Status: Common and abundant
Tools needed: None

The flowering dogwood tree makes spring in southern New England a visual treat. But sadly, extreme northern New England is too inhospitable for this cheery tree. There is a second best, though. That's bunchberry—a low-growing perennial with flowers that mimic its showier cousin. The flowers later become bright red edible berries that delight children young and old.

Summer is bunchberry time. The shiny red berries are ready slightly before other more notable berries come on the scene, and they last after the rest have withered on the vine.

Some authors refer to bunchberries as survival food, intimating that the taste is barely tolerable but anything that keeps meat on the bones is worth trying. I disagree with that assessment. To be candid, bunchberries are not delicious, nor are they overly sweet. But they have a mild flavor and are palatable enough to a hot, sweaty, and hungry person after a long walk through the woods. Bunchberries are not good enough to pick in great quantities and take home to freeze or to turn into jams and jellies. But for a quick pick-me-up, the ever-present bunchberry has a definite place as a trail nibble and is well worth discovering.

Bunchberries are low growing, never more than 6 or 8 inches tall. The leaves, which are widest in the middle and have a thin, pointed tip, are arranged in a whorl of six. The leaves are deeply veined and lack teeth. The showy, four-petaled (these are not true petals, but bracts—the actual flower is just the green disc in the center) blossoms are lime green early in the season and eventually turn a bright creamy white. The berries, naturally, grow in bunches.

WINTERGREEN
Gaultheria procumbens

Synonyms: Teaberry, checkerberry
Use: Trail nibble
Range: Throughout New England in open woodlands
Similarity to toxic species: Many plants with red berries are toxic; be sure of identification.
Best time: Year-round. Wintergreen berries persist over the winter, under the snow. In early spring they are literally the first wild edible of the season. The freezing process seems to make the "wintergreen" flavor more pronounced.
Status: Common and abundant
Tools needed: None

Collecting old-time medicine and extract bottles is one of my pet passions. These are fairly common around the old farms of New England, but a bottle with its label intact is an extraordinary find. One of my favorite bottles once held extract of wintergreen, and the somewhat yellowed label reads PURE ESSENCE CHECKERBERRY. FOR FLAVORING ICE CREAM, CUSTARDS, JELLIES, ICES, &C. DIRECTIONS: ONE-HALF TEASPOONFUL OR MORE TO A QUART ACCORDING TO THE TASTE. PREPARED BY N. WOOD AND SON, 428–430 FORE STREET, PORTLAND, ME. In the nineteenth and early twentieth centuries, Portland abounded with patent medicines and natural extract bottlers. And it is apparent that back then, people appreciated the penetrating flavor of wintergreen.

Today wintergreen is synthesized. No longer can we go to the local general store and purchase a bottle of "checkerberry extract." But we can still enjoy the rich taste and fragrance of wintergreen in its natural state. It is one of our more common woodland ground covers.

Look for thick mats of wintergreen in open woodlands. The shiny leaves are a little more than an inch long and have a few fine teeth. The color of the leaf varies from green to plum red. This variation of leaf color perplexed me until one blustery morning in early spring, when I happened to push a bunch of leaf litter aside with my boot. There before me was my answer: The leaves that had been covered with the litter were burgundy, but the leaves of neighboring plants, which were exposed to the light, were deep green. It would probably be possible to alter the color of any particular patch of wintergreen leaves simply by allowing or denying sunlight.

The small red berries are edible; so are the leaves. In fact, it is the leaves that I choose to chew on during my morning woodland perambulations. The leaves should not be swallowed, but when gently chewed they produce a perfectly wonderful wintergreen flavor, one the laboratory cannot quite duplicate.

The wintergreen flower is a tiny white bell, suspended by a thin U-shaped stem. The lip of the flower is gently scalloped. Wintergreen never gains more than an inch or so in height. The berries are unmistakable, though; if you are unsure of their identification, crushing a berry will yield that familiar wintergreen aroma.

In the dim past my grandmother used oil of wintergreen (along with lots of other potions and lotions, some of which I detested) on my young strains and muscle hurts. I can't remember if she diluted the stuff or not; probably she did, because it would be caustic if used straight from the bottle. Now every time I chew a wintergreen berry or nibble on a fragrant leaf, my grandma's tender ministrations come to mind, warm and comfortable. That's one of the nice things about plants—they can elicit fond memories. And what is nicer than that?

PURPLE TRILLIUM
Trillium undulatum

Synonyms: Red trillium, wake-robin, stinking Benjamin, birthroot
Uses: Cooked vegetable, salad ingredient
Range: Shaded woodlands throughout New England
Similarity to toxic species: None
Best time: May
Status: Locally abundant but rare in some locales. The biggest threat to purple trillium, as with so many other plants and animals, is not from foragers but from rampant development.
Tools needed: A jackknife or shears help snip the leaves.

A member of the lily family, purple trillium is a favorite wildflower, and although it is generally common and often occurs in large colonies, the species could potentially suffer from overeager foragers, especially in areas where it is scarce to begin with. Additionally, purple trillium is but one of many trilliums, some of which should never be picked. The careful forager might clip a leaf here and there from a colony of purple trilliums without doing the least bit of harm, but keep in mind that this plant should not be harvested in any quantity. Follow my lead and consider a dish of steamed purple trillium leaves a rite of spring, something special to look forward to each year.

Apparently conditions are just right for purple trilliums in the patch of woods along my driveway. The showy leaves and burgundy red flowers put on quite a show each spring. So here is where I harvest enough leaves for a side dish or two. I prefer purple trillium cooked rather than raw. Both are fine, though. Harvest by snipping only one leaf from each plant until you've gathered a sufficient amount. Don't pull up the entire plant.

For me, purple trillium means spring has sprung in all its glory. When the dark red, three-petaled flowers bloom, it is time to go fishing, for the mayfly hatches have surely begun. Ostrich fern fiddleheads are nearly past their prime, the warbler migration is ongoing, and it's time to do some serious work in the garden. And—in northern New England—the blackflies are out in force.

The leaves, petals, and sepals of purple trillium—indeed, all trilliums—occur in triplets. The plants stand between 6 and 16 inches tall, with the average about 8 inches. The leaves have a puckered shape, wide in the middle and with a tapering point at the end. If one leaf is picked, the remaining two look like a circus clown's outlandish bow tie.

Purple trilliums can also be tentatively identified by sniffing the flower, although I don't recommend this. Purple trillium is pollinated by flies and has the odor of rotten meat. Needless to say, it does not make a good cut flower.

Purple trillium, particularly the root, has a long history of medical uses, especially as a cure for menstrual cramps. However, any malady that purple trillium may ameliorate can be treated by other means. I discourage the folk-medicinal use of this pretty woodland plant.

TROUT LILY
Erythronium americanum

Synonyms: Dogtooth violet, adder's tongue
Use: Cooked vegetable
Range: Throughout New England
Similarity to toxic species: None
Best time: May
Status: Locally abundant but under siege by rampant development
Tools needed: None

For me, the distinction between trout lily, the plant, and trout, the fish, has long since become blurred. This has to do with the time that both come into their prime. May, in my part of Maine, brings with it a number of ephemeral plants—dainties of the woodlands that come and go, receiving only little notice from humans. Trout too, especially our native char, eastern brook trout, become invigorated at this time.

But the connection between brook trout and trout lily does not end with the happy coincidence of timing. Brook trout have wriggly vermiculations on their backs and lots of dots and speckles on their sides. To many, the general shape of trout lily leaves mimics the shape of a trout. And the markings on trout lily leaves certainly suggest the markings on a brook trout.

Trout lily leaves exhibit a relatively light shade of green and are mottled with brown splotches. The leaves, shaped like a lance head (or a brook trout), run between 4 and 10 inches long. Each plant has only two leaves; one of these usually stands nearly erect, while the other bends toward the horizontal.

The flowers, which sit atop a stem that is only slightly longer than the leaves, have six reflexed (bent back) yellow petals. I find the exact shade of yellow very similar to the color of the just-risen sun's rays as the light darts in my kitchen window and illuminates the floor. The backs of the petals exhibit a narrow strip of burgundy-brown.

Trout lilies can form expansive colonies consisting of thousands of individuals. Even before the flowers unfold, the great expanse of mottled leaves has a physical presence powerful enough to grab the attention of even the most disinterested observer.

Some years ago a roadside colony of trout lilies was doomed to fall beneath a bulldozer blade, so I rushed out and dug a number of plants. This was not an easy task, since the bulb-like corm lies far deeper than I had ever imagined. Nevertheless, diligence prevailed, and back home I went about setting out my trout lilies. It was a given that the top growth would not survive, but it seemed as though the corms had a good chance. I set them in a moist, shaded part of my lawn, and to my great pleasure, they survived. From that point on, my place had resident trout lilies.

As with some other edible but beautiful spring wildflowers, I was always reluctant to pick trout lilies for eating. But having read about the bulbs being tasty when boiled for ten minutes or so, I thought it worth trying. So it was on to another patch of trout lilies—a colony so large that digging several dozen corms would have no negative effect on the whole. But the effort was not worth the result. As noted earlier, the corms extend far, far down in the ground, and digging just one of the fingernail-diameter bulbs was way too much work. I got enough for my meal, though, and it was good.

The leaves are much easier to harvest. Still reluctant to destroy such a precious wildflower, I always make it a point to harvest only one leaf per plant. This does not appear to kill the plant, so my trout lily picking comes without any pangs of guilt.

Bear in mind that it is only the very young (best before the flowers open) leaves that make such a delightful potherb. Older leaves tend toward toughness. But that's okay, since trout lilies illustrate one of my often-repeated points regarding the forager's calendar year: Many plants have a short season or at least are only available in their prime for a brief time. That's okay too, since it makes such springtime delicacies all the more desirable. So appreciate early spring in New England for what it is: a time of beginnings, a time when nature awakens in a frenzied rush to bloom, reproduce, sow the seeds of new life. And, of course, spring is the time for foragers to pick a few bunches of trout lily leaves. Enjoy these special treats.

COMMON BLUE VIOLET
Viola papilionacea

Synonym: Violet
Uses: Trail nibble, salad ingredient, fancy syrup
Range: Throughout New England
Similarity to toxic species: None
Best time: May and June
Status: Common
Tools needed: None

The local woodpeckers tell me when it is time to pick wild violets. During the spring mating season, male woodpeckers woo the females by drumming on

RECIPE

Young violet leaves are excellent in salads. As might be expected of any dark green leaf, they are rich in vitamin A. My favorite use is in salads, but the leaves can also be boiled for a few minutes and served as a cooked vegetable.

anything that resonates, which can include barn doors, dead trees, aluminum boats, and metal roofs. This cacophony of sound coincides with prime violet-picking time.

Violets are not long lived when cut and placed in a small water-filled vase or jar. Even so, it is a rite of the season to grace the kitchen table with a fresh bouquet of these delicate wildflowers.

Violets range from 5 to 8 inches tall. The blossoms have five petals that show considerable venation. The leaves are somewhat heart shaped and are roughly toothed.

Besides being pretty, violet blossoms are eminently edible, even healthful—the dainty blue blossoms are packed with vitamin C. It's fun to pick handfuls of violet blossoms and munch on them while walking. Or the blossoms, minus the stems, can be added to any salad for taste as well as appearance. Want to surprise dinner guests? Place one perfect violet blossom in each cell of an ice cube tray, fill with water, freeze, and use in drinks. This is a real conversation piece and certainly more attractive than a cocktail onion or olive.

RECIPE

How about violet blossom syrup? Make a sugar syrup, using the same ratio—one part sugar to two parts water—used to fill a hummingbird feeder. Pour the hot syrup into a glass jar filled with violet blossoms. The violets relinquish their color, and streamers of blue can be seen swirling in the hot syrup. When all color has faded from the blossoms and the syrup has cooled, strain it, add a couple of good squirts of lemon juice, and place the jar in a dark cupboard. This syrup is a heavenly addition to crepes and pancakes. It also soothes scratchy throats and helps alleviate hoarseness.

SERVICEBERRY
Amelanchier spp.

Synonyms: Sarvisberry, Juneberry, shadberry
Uses: Trail nibble, frozen fruit, sauce, addition to muffins and pancakes
Range: Throughout New England
Similarity to toxic species: None
Best time: June and July
Status: Common
Tools needed: None

The study of the serviceberry presents many conflicting views and possibilities. It is variously estimated that between twenty and twenty-five species occur in North America, but hybridizing introduces additional variations. Fortunately all are similar in appearance, and all are more or less edible. Some are better than others.

The showy white blossoms, which look similar to cherry blossoms, are perhaps the best means of identifying the serviceberry. In very early spring, while patches of snow hold fast in the shaded woodland ravines and

FORAGER NOTE: During early spring it is easy to spot serviceberry in bloom while you're driving down the highway: It is the only thing blooming.

gullies, serviceberry puts on a dazzling display of pure white blossoms. These make a striking contrast to the still-drab browns and grays of the season.

In order to gain access to different sources of serviceberries, make note of the blooming plants in spring and revisit them in late June or early July, when the berries are ripe. When I encounter blooming serviceberries on my own property, I mark the spot with blue surveyor's flagging. I don't recommend doing this on the property of others, though.

Serviceberry occurs both as a tree and a shrub. Someone once determined that anything more than 20 feet tall was a tree; less than 20 feet, a shrub. Such strict distinctions are meaningless, though, when dealing with a tree/shrub that refuses to stay within formal boundaries. Fortunately it makes little difference, so long as the fruit is sweet and tasty.

Serviceberry has another admirable characteristic: Its wood is rock hard, one of the hardest on the continent. It is sometimes used for tool handles, but since the tree is of a small diameter, it cannot be used for furniture. The wood has a close grain and a handsome dark brown color with traces of red.

When serviceberry approaches the 20-foot mark, the limbs become whimsically contorted, with twists and turns of every description. Sometimes the lower limbs spread out horizontally only a few feet from the ground. A big serviceberry tree reminds me of Harry Lauder's walking stick. For those unfamiliar with Harry Lauder, he was a famous Scottish comedian and used a crooked walking stick as a prop.

Serviceberry leaves look much like apple leaves—finely toothed, somewhat leathery, and fairly thin. The leaves are alternate. The tight-fitting bark is medium gray. The berries, which are the real prize offered by the serviceberry, look much like blueberries. Early on the berries are purplish red; they later acquire the darkest shade of blue. Birds of every kind flock to ripe serviceberries, as do various

RECIPE

Serviceberries can be used fresh in muffins and pancakes. Or add the dried berries to pancake or muffin batter. They can also be used in old-fashioned, slow-cooking oatmeal.

small mammals and the young of the human species. Adults almost universally ignore the serviceberry's bounty, although in years past country folk of all ages paid homage to this lowly plant.

There is a great deal of variation in the flavor of serviceberries. It's odd that some trees have the sweetest berries imaginable, while the fruit of others is insipid, hardly fit for the birds. The key to finding good serviceberries is to sample every tree in the area.

Once a tree bearing delicious berries is located, the berries may be put to a variety of uses. First, and as you might guess, my favorite is to eat them as is. One serviceberry tree on the windward side of Cape Jellison, Maine, has the best-tasting fruit in the world (well, maybe not the world, but all of Maine anyway). To walk along the wild shore and gaze out at Penobscot Bay is pleasure enough, but add fresh, sweet serviceberries and the walk becomes a trip through a garden of earthly delights.

DRYING

Make a berry dryer of a roughly 36-by-24-inch nylon window screen fastened to a frame of wooden lathes. Attach screw eyes at the four corners, and suspend the frame from a beam in a dark attic, barn, or garage. Cover the screen with serviceberries, and check them every few days, moving them around a little by hand. Discard any berries that are mushy or unripe. When completely dried, store the berries in an airtight glass jar.

FREEZING

Use one part sugar to three parts berries. Freeze the berries in freezer jars.

Mushrooms

Eating wild mushrooms entails a degree of risk. The mushroom being collected must be positively identified as an edible variety. The consequences of a misidentification are too great to allow any room for error. A cavalier attitude has no place in the world of the wild-mushroom hunter.

To get a leg up on identifying and collecting wild mushrooms, learn everything there is to know about a single common variety. Become thoroughly knowledgeable about that particular mushroom. Then learn about another type. In time it will be possible to go afield and, if conditions are right, harvest a variety of delicious wild mushrooms.

New England, especially northern New England, because of its climate and forestation, is prime habitat for wild mushrooms, with hundreds of different kinds in residence. Of these, only a small number may be safely eaten.

No blanket statement can be made about mushroom habitat. Some, such as the various puffballs, seem to like a rather poor, gravelly soil. Others live on decaying trees and rotting stumps. And some like the acid ground so common around pinewoods. It is up to the collector to know the three Ws: what

FORAGER NOTE: Always clean wild mushrooms thoroughly, and always eat them cooked, not raw. Always.

kind of mushroom will be growing, when it will be prime, and where it will be found. After that, it's the same as anything else: Once you acquire knowledge, the subject is demystified.

Besides comparing a wild mushroom to a picture in a book and comparing features from a written description, a spore print usually must be taken in order to make a positive identification. The spores can be captured and examined by placing the mushroom—gill or pore side down—on a piece of paper and covering it with a drinking glass. Leave the mushroom overnight. The next day, lift it up; there will be a print of the spores.

Spore prints look much like a photographic negative (although in this case the print is a positive). Each mushroom has a different-color spore print. If the book says a certain mushroom leaves a brown spore print, use white paper; brown or black paper is better for a white spore print. Spore prints are things of beauty, wondrous pictures made by nature. Even if you don't eat mushrooms, it is great fun to make and collect spore prints.

Mushrooming requires much detailed concentration. To become completely knowledge-able, buy a guide that deals specifically with mushrooms. Also find a local mush-room club (they can be found in every state) and join. Go on field trips and take advantage of the club's collective experience.

I learned about mushrooms from friends and later made an in-depth study on my own. Now I am intimately familiar with a small number of mushrooms. These are the ones I purposely seek. I try to add to my stable of known varieties each year. The process is painstaking, though, because it involves consulting vari-ous field guides and taking spore prints. It is impossible to be too careful when dealing with wild mushrooms.

Be careful, take nothing for granted, and study, study, study. A door will then be opened to a remarkable new world of fasci-nating and often delicious wild plants. Happy hunting.

FORAGER NOTE: The few mushrooms listed here are by no means the only edible wild mushrooms native to New England. They are but a sample—a tiny example of the great range of mushrooms to be found in our region, chosen both for their esculence and ease of identifying them in the field.

FORAGER NOTE: Don't wash chan-terelles or any other mushrooms; this causes foreign matter to stick to them like glue. Instead, clean them dry. This may entail using a toothpick or even a small brush; a toothbrush works nicely. The tip of my jackknife also serves the purpose well.

Licensed by shutterstock.com

MOREL
Morchella esculenta

Synonym: Sponge mushroom
Use: Cooked
Range: Throughout New England
Similarity to toxic species: The false morel (*Gyromitra esculenta*) is sometimes mistaken for a true morel.
Best time: May
Status: Locally abundant; scarce in some areas
Tools needed: A knife helps sever the stem close to the ground.

Morels have been my Holy Grail in the mushroom world. Although I regularly searched for them, I never saw a wild morel near my Maine home until recently. A couple in a neighboring town, knowing my passion for wild mushrooms, called and asked me if I would like to come over and not only see but also pick a morel. I was in their driveway almost before they had a chance to hang up the phone.

The tension was considerable; this was a lifetime search about to be consummated. I was directed to a gravelly patch of lawn and told to poke about—a lone morel was there. And sure enough, after considerable crawling on my hands and knees, there it stood—a tiny, dark-gray mushroom, an honest-to-goodness morel. I examined every aspect of this storied fungus and then reverently slid my forefinger under the stem and popped it from the ground.

Back home the morel lost some of its mystery. I sliced it into four pieces to make it seem like more, and then sautéed it in butter. It was good—very good—as good as some of the more-common wild mushrooms I pick regularly around home. But it wasn't quite the religious experience I had hoped for.

Later another couple told me that their lawn was filled with morels; they had morels to spare, to wantonly fling to people like me. It struck me as odd that morels had been a will-o'-the-wisp to me for so long, while to these people the famed mushroom was no more special than an acorn.

Learn to distinguish between morels and false morels by noting the following characteristics: True morels have pits, and both the cap and stem are hollow. You can determine this by slicing lengthwise. False morels have folds, or convolutions, but are not pitted. The false morel looks sort of like a brain, whereas the true morel resembles a sponge.

A forager lucky enough to find a bunch of morel mushrooms might try the recipe on the previous page, courtesy of Ken Allen and taken from his book *Cooking Wild.* This recipe might be used for any mushrooms, not just morels.

RECIPE

If morels are scarce, which is more than likely, slice them lengthwise and gently and slowly cook in butter. This may take twenty minutes or more, but don't hurry the process.

CHICKEN OF THE WOODS
Laetiporus sulphureus

Synonym: Sulfur shelf
Use: Cooked
Range: Throughout New England
Similarity to toxic species: None
Best time: September and October
Status: Common
Tools needed: None required for picking, but chicken of the woods often occurs in huge quantities; bring a cardboard box or large canvas sack to hold the bounty.

I've been told that chicken of the woods gets its name from its flavor—it's said to taste like chicken. I know a few things that taste like chicken, but this isn't one of them. Still, properly sautéed in butter, chicken of the woods does taste a little like lobster. But lobsters don't live in the woods, and maybe that's why the anonymous mycophile who named this mushroom chose chicken instead. The flesh is meaty, though, much like lobster flesh.

Chicken of the woods is a shelf mushroom and grows on injured or dying hardwood trees. It isn't uncommon, but in my area it has the maddening habit of growing best in the yards of people who never pick the stuff themselves but won't allow others the privilege. Chicken of the woods also grows on wooded property, generally where every other tree is posted with intimidating NO TRESPASSING signs. These signs rarely carry the name of the landowner, so it's impossible to call or visit and seek permission to pick the mushroom. Once in a great while, a colony of chicken of the woods is spotted on land where public access is allowed. These are places to remember.

One fall during a futile wild-cranberry expedition, I pulled my canoe ashore, sat on a log, and marveled at the striking brilliance of the fall foliage around the surrounding wetland and nearby hardwood ridges. It was enough to be alive and well on such a day, to be immersed in this kaleidoscope of color. Then, as if in reward for a humble attitude, I looked behind me and there, on a dead black cherry tree, was a huge chicken of the woods mushroom. Suddenly cranberries didn't matter a whit. Nature had provided.

FORAGER NOTE: Chicken of the woods often appears on the same site, year after year. However—and this is worth noting—it doesn't always appear at the same time. My records indicate as much as a three-week spread from one year to the next. Temperature, humidity, and rainfall have much to do with the emergence of this colorful fungus. This means that once you locate a site, you should visit it regularly during the fruiting season. It doesn't take long for the mushroom to appear, reach its prime, and then dry to inedibility. Such diligent monitoring is worthwhile, however; this is one of the very finest mushrooms available.

RECIPE

Chicken of the woods can be slowly simmered in butter and served as is. Like hen of the woods, chicken of the woods must be chopped into manageable bits and thoroughly rinsed to remove any bark, wood fibers, or insects. If the mushroom is slightly older than might be hoped, the outer edge will be the most tender. Save this portion separately from the rest to be used for frying and in fritters. If it's not too tough, the rest can be chopped fine and used in stews. The long, slow cooking helps tenderize the mushroom. I retain all but the toughest portions of chicken of the woods because the flavor is so satisfying, even if the mushroom is a bit chewy.

Once picked, chicken of the woods stores well in the refrigerator crisper.

Chicken of the woods is so easily identified that it is a perfect "beginner" mushroom. It's a bracket-type mushroom and grows in giant clusters. The bottom of the cap has pores rather than gills, and the top is smooth and somewhat fluted. The margins are slightly wavy. The color is usually bright orange, running toward a creamy yellow on the edges. The style and color of chicken of the woods make it recognizable even to those who would not otherwise eat a wild mushroom. This makes it a highly desired product for sale at health food stores, where the cut-up mushroom is peddled at ridiculously high prices.

HEN OF THE WOODS
Grifola frondosa

Use: Cooked
Range: Throughout New England
Similarity to toxic species: None
Best time: September and October
Status: Common
Tools needed: A knife will help cut the base of the mushroom from the host stump, but the mushroom can also be picked by hand.

A lone oak stump on a gravel road in the rolling hills of Midcoast Maine once hosted spores of the hen of the woods mushroom. Each fall some friends who live just down the road from this treasure trove would call me when the mushrooms were at their prime, and we would pick pounds of the rubbery polypore.

But our annual hen of the woods harvest was soon to be a thing of the past. The local snowplow man was annoyed because his plow blade often came up short on the mushroom stump. So the following spring a backhoe dug out all traces of the stump. And that fall, when we should have reveled in many pounds of hen of the woods, there were none to be found.

Hen of the woods is excellent fried. This is one mushroom that needs to be fried for more than just a few minutes. You don't need to cook it to a crisp, but give it at least fifteen minutes of slow cooking. Add half an ounce of sherry and perhaps a dash of Angostura bitters to the pan during cooking, per your preference.

Since then another stump along another road has provided us with our hen of the woods. Eventually that stump too will be history and we will have to find an alternate source. But that's mushrooming.

Hen of the woods looks rather like a big, brown coral. The chestnut-brown, cream-streaked caps are attached to a thick, fleshy base. The tops of the caps are relatively smooth, with minute pores located on the undersides. The mushroom has a rubbery texture.

The hen of the woods and a similar mushroom called many-capped polypore (*G. umbellata*) are nearly identical in appearance, and both are perfectly edible. Both are common in New England.

This mushroom needs some preparation before being eaten or preserved. Hen of the woods must be cut up into fairly small pieces—say, half the size of the average potato chip—because it is somewhat tough. That accomplished, the list of what you can do with this versatile mushroom is practically endless.

Sometime next September begin the search for a stump that harbors hen of the woods mushrooms. With luck, the site should produce for many years— unless the local snowplow man develops a grudge against it.

FREEZING

Hen of the woods freezes well. Simply sauté the mushrooms in butter or margarine, allow them to cool, and then put them in plastic freezer bags.

Hen of the woods is also a superior soup and stew ingredient, imparting both an interesting texture and a slightly bitter taste that contrasts wonderfully with the other ingredients. Any casserole can benefit by the addition of half a cup of chopped hen of the woods.

CANNING

But what about folks who must not eat fried foods? The answer came to me recently when I had a big supply of hen of the woods and, being gun-shy about putting an entire year's supply of mushrooms in the freezer (the electrical power grid where I live is not dependable, and a few years ago I lost nearly my whole freezer of food during an ice storm), I decided to see if the mushrooms would benefit from home canning. They did.

I packed the mushrooms in good old well water and processed them according to the pressure canner's instructions. The finished product was actually more flavorful than the fried mushrooms. And the slight bitter taste inherent in hen of the woods? Gone.

RECIPE

Scrambled eggs with hen of the woods mushrooms is a breakfast treat that people would fight over. (An Italian friend tells me that in Italy, violence has erupted over proprietary rights to prime hen of the woods sites.) First fry the mushrooms; when they are tender, pour in two beaten eggs. Stir until the eggs are cooked, and serve with any good Louisiana hot sauce. Mercy, it's good. Omelets can also be elevated to the heavenly realm when you add hen of the woods to the mix.

GIANT PUFFBALL
Calvatia gigantea (and other *Calvatia* species)

GEM-STUDDED PUFFBALL
Lycoperdon perlatum

Use: Cooked
Range: Throughout New England
Similarity to toxic species: A careless collector might confuse the developing *Amanita phalloides,* a highly toxic species, with a puffball.
Best time: September and October
Status: Common and abundant
Tools needed: None

Every child intuitively knows how puffball mushrooms got their name. Step on a ripe one and out puffs a cloud of "smoke." Puffball flesh eventually changes to dark brown spores; it is these spores that produce the dense cloud when the puffball is stepped on or agitated.

Only immature puffballs—those whose flesh has not yet turned to spores—with pure white flesh are edible. The majority of puffballs fall within this wide category, but there is an exception. The hard-skinned puffball (*Scleroderma citrinum*) has purplish-black flesh except when very young; later it has white flesh.

This hard-skinned variety is easy to spot, even without examining the flesh; no other puffball has a textured, warty surface. Besides the rough, hard surface and the black interior, the hard-skinned puffball is denser and weighs more than other puffballs of the same size. It is easy to recognize and therefore easy to avoid.

The acid test of any puffball is to slice it lengthwise and look at the exposed flesh. If the vague form of a cap-style mushroom is evident, it may be a young amanita. Cap-style mushrooms have a stem, however, and since there is no true stem on a puffball (it has roots instead, and is puckered on the bottom), the difference should be readily apparent. If the puffball half exhibits pure white flesh that is the consistency of cheese, it is a good one.

Once you learn to identify a puffball, it is easy to spot them even from far away. Indeed, they are perfect beginner mushrooms because they are so easy to identify. One of my preferred modes of hunting giant puffballs is to slowly drive down what I call "puffball alley"—a stretch of country road that hosts great numbers of puffballs each year. It's lazy man's mushrooming; all I have to do is stop, get out of the car, pick the mushroom, and drive on. Besides along the roadsides, look for puffballs, both the giant kind and the gem-studded type, on the poorest land around—on old lawns that have never been fertilized, on gravelly lots, and even around the edge of gravel pits.

Puffballs literally come up overnight. When I was a boy, a giant puffball the size of a jumbo loaf of bread once magically appeared on our back lawn. The old farmer down the road wanted it, and Grandpa let him have it. Grandpa was afraid of mushrooms and didn't dare experiment with them—a wise move on his part, in view of his lack of knowledge of the different fungi.

Of the two groups of puffballs featured in this entry, the gem-studded variety is my favorite. Gem-studded puffballs are particularly easy to spot because of two features. First, they are covered with lots of small, rubbery spines (the

RECIPE

The easiest way to prepare puffballs is to slice them in half and fry them in butter or margarine. For folks who don't want to use butter or margarine, simmer the fresh or frozen puffballs in chipotle sauce. This is a low-heat chili sauce made from vinegar, molasses, onions, chipotle chilies, and olive oil. Mostly used as a barbecue or steak sauce, it works well for frying mushrooms because it doesn't scorch and stick to the pan. You can substitute any similar steak or barbecue sauce that exhibits similar properties. But since gem-studded puffballs are somewhat mild, the chilies and other flavors in a chipotle sauce transport these mushrooms from simply good to the realm of magnificent.

"gems") that are easily rubbed off with a finger. The second feature is the unique pear shape. With only a modest stretch of the imagination, you might say these fungi are minaret shaped. Gem-studded puffballs rarely exceed 1 inch in width (this being at the top, the widest part) and perhaps 2 inches in height.

Often these mushrooms grow in solid drifts, where it is possible to pick several quarts in a few minutes. Whenever I run across such a jackpot, the question of what's for dinner is rendered moot. Whatever else is on the menu, gem-studded puffballs will take center stage.

Both gem-studded puffballs and giant puffballs are early-season mushrooms. Begin searching for them in late August, especially after a wet spell.

FREEZING

To prepare gem-studded puffballs for freezing, slice them in half and simmer in plain water. They can later be fried in the medium of choice, placed in freezer bags or containers, and frozen. You don't have to thaw mushrooms before cooking, as long as they are allowed to simmer over low heat. Talk about fast food!

Giant puffballs also can be frozen, but the taste becomes too strong for my liking.

Remedy: *Nearly every old-time New England farmer knew to collect mature puffballs—the kind that puff when squeezed—in fall. These were stored in strategic spots around the barn. When an animal cut itself, the farmer would grab a puffball, aim it at the wound, and squeeze. The spores have styptic properties and stop all but the worst bleeding. They are also sterile and help ward off infection.*

OYSTER MUSHROOM
Pleurotus ostreatus

Use: Cooked
Range: Throughout New England
Similarity to toxic species: None
Best time: October and November
Status: Locally abundant
Tools needed: None

The oyster mushroom is so called because it is shaped like an oyster shell, not because it tastes like oysters (which it doesn't). This is one of my favorite mushrooms because of its sweet, satisfying flavor. Unfortunately mushrooms are not the most dependable crop; some years oyster mushrooms fail to emerge in any appreciable numbers.

Oyster mushrooms grow on dead trees and old, rotting stumps. They begin as tiny white specks in early October and by mid-November are an inch or so wide. This is a scale-type mushroom; the gills are on the bottom, facing the ground. A colony of oyster mushrooms is often tightly packed, with individuals alongside, above, and below one another in layers. The top of the creamy white "oyster" has a waxy feel.

A deep glen at the far end of my woodlot is home to a couple of colonies of oyster mushrooms. One of these is on its way out—the stump the oysters live on is almost completely rotted and returned to the ground. The other colony is on a relatively intact stump. These mushrooms need to be carefully monitored so they can be harvested at the peak of perfection.

This gives me a good excuse to take shotgun in hand and, with the best of intentions, walk "out back" for a few grouse and a mess of mushrooms. In truth, I've only hit the grouse-mushroom jackpot once. My aging bird dog, Ben, flushed a beautiful male ruffed grouse and I made a picture-perfect shot. Ben fetched the grouse, which I stuffed in the game pouch of my canvas hunting coat. Then, without moving more than a few feet, I knelt down and harvested several pounds of perfect oyster mushrooms. It just doesn't get any better than that.

But now Ben is gone and the oyster mushroom colony has lost its vigor. It's time for me to move on, time to find another stump or dead tree that hosts a colony of sweet, mild oyster mushrooms.

If I had to make a choice between oyster mushrooms and morels, I would always choose the oysters, hands down. That's how good they are!

RECIPE

Carefully clean the mushrooms (bits of the dead stump might be attached at the stem, and specks of debris might be trapped in the gills). Without further preparation, gently sauté them in butter, being careful not to let them brown too much.

CHANTERELLE
Cantharellus cibarius

Use: Cooked
Range: Throughout New England
Similarity to toxic species: *C. cibarius* could potentially be mistaken for the toxic *Omphalotus olearius*, or jack-O'-lantern mushroom. However, the jack-O'-lantern's thin, closely set gills and tendency to grow in clusters separate it from chanterelles.
Best time: July through September; occasionally into October
Status: Common and locally abundant
Tools needed: None

My Midcoast Maine woodlot has everything chanterelles need. A combination of deciduous and evergreen trees, along with regenerating openings and a rich base of woodland loam, make my place a haven for these orange-yellow mushrooms. In fact, they grow so thickly that by late summer, I begin to tire of them. And that's saying something, because chanterelles number among the tastiest of wild mushrooms.

Since chanterelles are so delicious and abundant, I include them here despite their very slight resemblance to the toxic jack-O'-lantern. But once you learn to positively identify chanterelles, the chance of confusing them with anything else disappears.

First of all, remember that chanterelles grow singly, one here and one there. The forager may encounter a small patch of woodland that hosts a great number of chanterelles, but close inspection will reveal that they grow one at a time, never in clusters or clumps.

Next remember that jack-O'-lanterns grow on or near wood. This can include not only dead logs and windfalls but also the base of live trees and even buried logs and stumps. Chanterelles, on the other hand, grow out of the woodland loam.

Also, while chanterelles exhibit a pretty combination of orange and yellow, jack-O'-lanterns are bright, almost garish, orange.

Chanterelles have distinctive ridges, or gills. These are quite wide apart and also run part of the way down the stalk, or stem. The ridges are forked, being wider apart as they approach the cap and closer together at the opposite end.

Chanterelles have a smooth, nearly flat cap. This may become depressed in the center on mature specimens. The top of the cap feels dry or perhaps a bit waxy to the touch.

Jack-O'-lantern mushrooms have bioluminescent gills. (To observe this, place an upturned specimen in a dark room or closet.) Finally, jack-O'-lanterns have a sweetish, somewhat unpleasant odor. Some field guides list chanterelles as having the scent of apricots, but that has never been apparent to me.

Look for chanterelles in mixed-growth woodland in summer. Make sure to only pick them if the mushrooms are growing singly and if the ridges or gills appear as described here. Once you've positively identified chanterelles, prepare for some delicious eating.

Chanterelles don't just come up in one flush and then disappear. They keep coming as long as sufficient rainfall triggers their growth.

RECIPE

Cut the chanterelles into smaller pieces so that they will cook through all at the same time. In a cast-iron frying pan, since it imparts such even heat, melt half a stick (one-quarter cup) of butter. (Canola oil is a good substitute after enjoying several meals of chanterelles.) Drop the cut-up chanterelles in the pan, and stir frequently. The mushrooms are done when they begin to brown on the edges. Serve immediately, piping hot.

Leftover cooked chanterelles keep for a day or so if placed on a plate and covered with aluminum foil or clear plastic wrap.

So what do we do with a handbasket (the best way to keep mushrooms in the field) filled to the brim with chanterelles? Upon arriving home, spread the mushrooms out on a table and inspect them for clinging debris or insects.

Clean, dry mushrooms can last in the refrigerator for several days. If storing in a plastic bag, don't close the bag, which can cause the mushrooms to sweat.

I like to use the year's first big batch of chanterelles as the main course for a wild meal. This may include garden "weeds" such as lamb's-quarters and perhaps a serving of purslane.

The first hard frost of autumn puts an end to my chanterelle-fest. It is with some degree of sadness that I bid farewell to these abundant, dependable, and delicious wild mushrooms. My solace lies in anticipation of yet another season spent walking the New England woods, picking chanterelles.

FREEZING

Chanterelles freeze well. Prepare as if for immediate use (see below), and then place on a dinner plate or in a bowl and allow to cool. Oil works better than butter for chanterelles you're going to freeze. Olive oil is good, but canola is cheaper and also heart-healthy. Place the cooked, somewhat-cooled chanterelles in plastic sandwich bags. Fold over the top of the bag and squeeze out any air. Place as many of these chanterelle-filled bags as will fit into a ziplock freezer bag. Don't place the cooked mushrooms directly in a freezer bag—they will soon become freezer burned, dry and tasteless.

BLACK TRUMPET
Craterellus cornucopioides

Synonyms: Horn of plenty, death trumpet, hornlike craterellus
Use: Cooked
Range: Widespread, not only in New England but also throughout the entire Northern Hemisphere
Similarity to toxic species: None
Best time: August and September
Status: Common, widespread and abundant
Tools needed: None

With a common name like "death trumpet," how could this uniquely shaped mushroom rate as choice? Common names often do a grievous disservice to a perfectly useful, safe, and delicious wild-food product. My lifelong association with black trumpets was founded on a total misconception. As a child, old-timers often warned me away from "death trumpets," and I did so until adulthood. Had I known the scientific name of black trumpets and connected it with the horn of plenty, or cornucopia, I might have enjoyed many additional years of harvesting and eating this great mushroom.

After discovering this mushroom in a tattered volume on wild mushrooms, I immediately recognized it as the one that I had avoided all my life. A feeling of chagrin swept over me as I read how this was a choice, edible mushroom. Still, better safe than sorry.

It didn't take long to discover that *C. cornucopioides* was present on my Maine woodlot. Imagine the thrill of finding a huge swath of these mushrooms in the middle of an unused woods road on my property. It took only a short time to fill a large basket. My taste buds practically tingled with anticipation of a new and delicious wild offering.

My first meal of black trumpets had to wait while I cleaned my bounty. These, like all mushrooms, must be hand cleaned. That amounts to separating the mushrooms from clinging bits of moss, sticks, and leaf litter—a tedious but not entirely unpleasant task.

From midsummer on, look for stands of trumpet-shaped black mushrooms, many only 1 inch tall, others up to 3 or 4 inches tall. Black trumpets are sometimes likened to an inverted cow's horn, a very accurate analogy. The body of the trumpet is quite thin, and the outside sports rudimentary gills in the form of slight ridges. Not all black trumpets are black. A single stand of these mushrooms can feature black, light brown, and even gray individuals. All are good.

Like chanterelles, black trumpets have a long growing season, with flushes of them appearing shortly after nearly every soaking rain. In fact, the season

RECIPE

For your first meal of black trumpets, choose butter rather than oil as a cooking medium. Drop half a stick (one-quarter cup) of butter into a cast-iron frying pan, heat set on low. Introduce the whole mushrooms, as well as bits and pieces of torn ones. These pieces quickly cook down rather than soak up the melted butter, and appear to add to the liquid content of the frying pan. This blackish liquid is actually a delicious nectar—an extremely flavorful mushroom gravy. The mushrooms and accompanying sauce go delightfully well over a serving of jasmine rice.

I can't recall what accompanied my first meal of black trumpet mushrooms, but the taste, texture, and even the sight of my initial meal of these delicate mushrooms stands etched in my memory.

lasts far longer than I had imagined. Strolling past a place on my woodlot where black trumpets had previously flourished, I saw a new batch of them. This was in late September, after it seemed to me that all the black trumpets had long-since disappeared. Interestingly, these late-season mushrooms were significantly larger than those that appeared in July and August.

FREEZING

Black trumpets freeze well. While I'm writing this, a storage container filled with sautéed trumpets sits in my freezer, awaiting cooking on New Year's Day.

SPREADING HYDNUM
Dentinum repandum

Synonym: The British know this as hedgehog fungus.
Use: Cooked
Range: Throughout New England
Similarity to toxic species: None
Best time: August and September
Status: Common and widespread
Tools needed: None

Examine a photo of this mushroom and you'll see the small, spinelike projections covering the bottom of the cap. From that it's pretty easy to associate the first part of the scientific name, *Dentimum*, with "dental." Indeed, the thin, pointed spines do somewhat resemble sharp little teeth.

This thick, meaty mushroom ranks among my very favorites. I covet its mild flavor and firm texture. I'm always happy to give friends and acquaintances samples of my wild foods, but when it comes to spreading hydnums, my generosity becomes somewhat reserved.

Spreading hydnums grow happily in both deciduous and coniferous forests, as well as in the mixed-growth forest so typical of Maine and other New

England states. Beginning in midsummer—sometime in early August in Midcoast Maine—look for small scatterings of 2-inch-tall mushrooms with stout stalks and a dry, sometimes scaly cap with spiny projections covering the bottom. The top of the cap has the curious color combination found in those popular orange-

FORAGER NOTE: Don't look for spreading hydnums in the deep, dark woods. Rather, seek them where filtered sunlight penetrates the forest canopy. This holds true for a great many edible wild mushrooms.

vanilla ice-cream bars. While I would be the last one to suggest yet another common name for any plant, I privately refer to spreading hydnums as "Creamsicle mushrooms" because of the color of the cap.

These mushrooms grow in soil, often near decomposing logs and, according to some authorities, near the roots of larch trees. I have yet to find a spreading hydnum near any of the many larches on my property, however.

It pays to become as familiar as possible with any new mushroom, so here are two ways in addition to color to help you identify spreading hydnum: First, the cap readily breaks from the stalk. This frequently happens when the mushrooms are carelessly dropped into a basket or canvas shopping bag. Second, the "teeth," or projections, on the bottom of the cap are readily rubbed off by just gentle pressure from a finger.

My introduction to this fine table mushroom came when, having studied the species in a bulletin put out by the University of Maine Cooperative Extension Service, I spotted several spreading hydnums on a secluded corner of my woodlot. These mushrooms grew along a line delineated by a mostly decomposed white ash tree. I immediately recognized the mushrooms. Still, I made it

RECIPE

Cooking methods for spreading hydnums are the same as for any other mushroom described here. However, I never have enough of these delicacies to warrant doing anything other than sautéing the fresh, cut-up caps and stalks. And believe me, I never have any left over. These fine mushrooms are a meal unto themselves, more than sufficient for the hungriest forager.

Clean your spreading hydnums by brushing off any clinging debris; either do this by hand or with a small brush. Then chop into small pieces and sauté in oil or butter. Cook only until mushroom bits are fork tender.

a point to inspect the teeth and also take note of the overall appearance of cap and stalk.

For many years the bulk of my spreading hydnums came from the one spot. Only occasionally did I find the same species in other areas. So last year, when only three or four smallish mushrooms appeared at the appointed time and place, it looked as though my stand was dwindling, and in only a few years there would be no more spreading hydnums.

Much later in fall, after several severe frosts had destroyed all mushrooms, I found several frost-killed but very large spreading hydnums in an entirely different area of the woodlot. Marking the place down in my mind, I intend to visit again next summer in hopes of finding more of these, one of my all-time favorite mushrooms.

Plants of Swamps, Bogs, and Slow-Moving Streams

Some plants must grow where it is wet, some on the moist ground, and some in the water. Marsh marigolds, cattails, pickerelweed, and wild cranberries represent only a sample of such moisture-loving plants.

Every bog or sluggish stream in New England hosts at least some useful plants. Sometimes such areas are not easily visited. Hip boots, even a boat or canoe, are needed to get to where the plants grow. But these places are a different world from what we are used to. Besides the plants, various fish, insects, birds, and amphibians make swamps, bogs, and sluggish streams home. Even in the midst of industrial and urban areas, the wet spots offer a home to a plethora of interesting plants and animals. The forager cherishes such places for the beauty and diversity they represent.

CATTAIL
Typha latifolia

Synonym: Cat-o'-nine-tail
Uses: Trail nibble, cooked vegetable, flour additive, salad ingredient
Range: Widespread throughout New England
Similarity to toxic species: None
Best time: At their best and easiest to harvest in spring, summer, and fall; available as emergency food in winter
Status: Common
Tools needed: To dig roots in early spring, a hand trowel or garden spade is helpful, as is a jackknife to cut the sprouts and later the young shoots and flower spikes.

Kids and cattails go together. Whether it's using the dried flower heads as torches or shaking the stalk so the wind sets the downy seeds adrift, the common cattail has a magnetic appeal to young ones. Perhaps the cattail's preferred location—wet areas, with the accompanying life forms such as frogs, dragonflies, and noisy red-winged blackbirds—adds to the plant's universal attraction. What better wild-food plant might anyone choose to introduce a child to the art of foraging?

Eating cattails is not a New England tradition, at least among the

FORAGER NOTE: Cattail shoots, or stalks, are similar in style to a leek. They grow in layers, with the outer layer being tough and the inner layers tender and delicate.

European community. For Native Americans, however, it's a different story. I once watched, spellbound, as a member of Maine's Penobscot tribe taught a group of youngsters how to find, prepare, and eat cattail stalks during a living-history demonstra-

FORAGER NOTE: Don't worry about harming a stand of cattails by harvesting them. Harvesting stimulates rather than hinders growth.

tion. The kids also got to ride in a real birch-bark canoe and visit a shelter sheathed in birch bark. The cattails, though, seemed to make the biggest impression. And whether those children ever make a traditional Native American shelter or attempt to fashion a birch-bark canoe later in life, they will always know how to eat a cattail.

Cattails, both the common and the narrow-leaved variety (*T. angustifolia*), have a multitude of uses throughout the growing season. In early spring, when ice still clings to the edges of small ponds and the first wood frog bravely utters its initial staccato croak of the season, the first cattail product is ready for harvest. These are the dormant sprouts, which if not picked will produce another crop of cattails. The sprouts range up to 1 inch long, are white and smooth, and are shaped like the spur on a rooster's foot.

To harvest the cattail sprouts requires some determination. Knee-length rubber boots are a must, for it is usually necessary to wade out into the still-icy water and pull the old, dead cattail clumps from the protesting muck. The sprouts are attached at the ends of the roots and may be removed by hand but are best severed with a jackknife. They may be rinsed in clean water and eaten raw, tossed in a salad (my favorite use), or steamed or boiled until tender and used as a cooked vegetable. Cattail sprouts make an interesting addition to the usual bean sprouts in an Oriental stir-fry. Harvesting a mess of cattail sprouts is an invigorating way to welcome spring.

The next cattail product is available in late spring, when the plants are from 1 to 3 feet high. These are the young shoots (immature stalks). While they can be pulled from the mud by hand, it is much easier to cut them at the base of the plant. The shoots then need to be trimmed in order to expose the pure white stalk inside.

After the cattail plant reaches maturity, it offers yet another food product: the cattail itself, which is really the pistillate, or female flower spike. The staminate, or male flower spike, is located directly above the female, giving a two-layered appearance. It is the more substantial, female flower spike that serves the forager now.

RECIPE

Slice cattail shoots into short lengths and use them as the main ingredient in a unique stir-fry. For a fine cooked vegetable, boil or steam the shoots for ten minutes; drain and serve with butter, salt, and pepper.

The cigar-shaped flower spike can be eaten over quite a long period but is best harvested when the surface can be easily crumbled with the thumbnail. If the flower spike is picked while still encased in its parchment-like sheath, it will be a bit tough and somewhat insipid. Use the thumbnail test to determine readiness and then, using a jackknife, cut as many flower spikes as needed.

For the cattail's final product, the flower spikes eventually become coated with a thick layer of yellow pollen. To gather the pollen, bend the flower spike over a large paper bag and give it a sharp tap. Clouds of pollen will fall into the bag. At home, spread the pollen out on a clean newspaper to allow any insects the opportunity to depart. Store it in a closed container.

One of my favorite cattail marshes recently fell victim to a shopping center. By design or by accident, the developers left part of the marsh intact. Now I park in a paved parking lot and pick my cattail spikes within a stone's throw of my car. I wonder what shoppers think the weird guy with hip boots and canvas bag is doing in that "nasty" swamp?

FREEZING

Mature cattails freeze well and keep for a year or more. To freeze cattail seed stalks, blanch for two minutes and cool immediately by placing in cold water. Then place in plastic freezer bags and store in the freezer.

Trail food: *Young cattail shoots are a wonderfully versatile vegetable. Because they can be eaten raw, immediately after picking, they qualify as a trail nibble.*

EXTRA RECIPE

Add cattail pollen, on a half-and-half basis, to wheat flour. It imparts an interesting flavor and pretty color to pancakes, biscuits, and muffins. Or use it to coat fish fillets before frying. Be innovative; that's half the fun of dealing with wild foods.

PICKERELWEED
Pontederia cordata

Uses: Trail nibble, cereal ingredient, cooked vegetable
Range: Throughout New England
Similarity to toxic species: None
Best time: May through September
Status: Common and abundant
Tools needed: None

Although my grandpa told me early on that this abundant weed was edible, we never picked any. Every time we encountered pickerelweed, we were engrossed in another pursuit: bass fishing.

One September many years later, I recalled that the flower spikes were covered with little nutlike seeds. I tried a handful and wasn't awfully impressed.

RECIPE

Pickerelweed leaves can be used as a potherb and are best gathered when young, before they unfurl. Boil for ten minutes, drain, and serve with butter, salt, and pepper.

They tasted good enough but did not inspire me. All the same, I picked enough to take home and dry.

The dried seeds are a different story: nutty and pleasantly crunchy. They are good as out-of-hand nibbles or can be added to any dry cereal or to a granola mixture.

Mature pickerelweed has smooth, dark green, arrowhead-shaped leaves. In summer the flower spikes are covered with pretty little violet-blue flowers. These must be rubbed off before eating the nutty seeds. Pickerelweed grows in profuse colonies along the edges of slow-moving streams and in shallow, weedy ponds.

WILD CRANBERRY
Vaccinium macrocarpon

Uses: Sauce, jelly, juice, relish, stuffing, muffin ingredient
Range: Throughout New England
Similarity to toxic species: None
Best time: September
Status: Common
Tools needed: None

Wild cranberries are about the same size and shape, and taste the same, as the commercially raised variety. The difference is that the wild cranberries are free. Early fall in a New England cranberry bog is a time of brilliant, contrasting colors; consider taking your camera along on your foraging expedition.

RECIPE

Cranberries can also be used in standard jelly and relish recipes. The resulting product is colorful and tangy.

A sluggish, winding stream bisects my favorite cranberry bog, and an old 17-foot fiberglass White brand canoe is my ticket to this magical place. Since an independent electric power producer now controls this stream, the cranberries are hit or miss. Some years there's too much water; other years, not enough. But in the years the dam owner manages not to harm the berries, it's time to gather gallons of the tart red fruits. This bog was once commercially harvested, but now only die-hard foragers like me venture out in search of cranberries.

In Maine mid-September is the time to pick cranberries. Most are almost but not quite ripe at this time. That's fine, because the unripe berries will slowly ripen in a cardboard box at home, much like a partially green tomato. It is easy to pick a few gallons of berries with your fingers.

The wild cranberry is a vining plant, with short, alternate, paddle-shaped leaves. The berries are about ½ inch or less in diameter. When ripe they may retain a trace of yellow, but this does not hurt their flavor. Fully ripe or overripe fruits are a dark red.

Cranberries can be stored in a cool place for many weeks. If many of the berries are only about half red, it is a good idea to check them every other day, removing the ripe berries and separating them from the rest.

Although September is cranberry month in New England, it is possible to find overwintered cranberries in early spring. These carryover cranberries are soft but still edible, and I eat a few raw when I find them. They're a greeting from a past season, a sign of the continuing flow of nature's bounty.

DRYING

Cranberries can be dried by placing on a drying rack made of a wooden frame and nylon window screen (don't use metal screening, as it may cause a chemical reaction with food products). Hang the screen in a cool, airy place for at least one week and perhaps longer, depending upon ambient humidity. When dry the berries will be light and somewhat shriveled. Store in an airtight container.

FREEZING

Cranberries keep well in the freezer, literally for years. To freeze cranberries, first rinse them. Allow the berries to dry and then put them in freezer bags. No blanching is required.

WILD MINT
Mentha arvensis

Synonyms: Brook mint, peppermint
Uses: Seasoning, tea ingredient, aromatherapy
Range: Throughout New England
Similarity to toxic species: None
Best time: May through September
Status: Abundant and widespread
Tools needed: None

Mint is mint, isn't it? Not necessarily. Our native mint varies greatly in strength from one location to another. So if one location produces mint of only so-so strength, try looking elsewhere.

Wild mint grows abundantly along streams, brooks, rivers, ponds, and lakes; in perennially wet areas; and even along roadside ditches. This makes it one of the most abundant and easily located of all edible wild plants.

Everyone has tasted or at least smelled some form of mint. But those who have never tried wild mint have a delightful experience awaiting them. For me, wild mint long ago supplanted any of the weaker-flavored cultivated varieties.

Wild mint ranks as my favorite scented herb, fresh or dried. However, when mint is dried, the essential oil becomes concentrated, making the mint far more potent and aromatic. Placed in a sealed container, crushed dried wild mint has a longer shelf life than any other aromatic herb I can think of. Even two-year-old mint comes alive when rubbed over leg of lamb or sprinkled inside the body cavity of a fresh trout or salmon.

When hunting streamsides and similar places for wild mint, don't expect to find huge, striking plants. Instead, most wild mint plants stand no more than 24 inches tall; some are only half that.

The leaves grow opposite each other, in pairs. As with all members of the mint family, the stem is squared rather than round. Little clusters of tiny blue flowers grow in the leaf axils, that place where the leafstalk joins the main stalk.

The biggest aid to identifying wild mint is, of course, that unmistakable mint aroma. Just brush or bruise a plant that meets the above description; if it is wild mint, you will immediately notice a strong aroma of mint.

When gathering my wild mint last summer, I accidentally pulled some plant material up by the roots. This seemed a good chance to try growing wild mint at home. It was too late in the year for setting outside, so I rooted my mint in a jar of water. Little white rootlets formed within days. The plants were then transplanted to a hanging flowerpot, which I hung in front of my south-facing glass door. My wild mint has become well established, and I delight in brushing it with my hand and sniffing it—aromatherapy in its most basic form.

One of my favorite uses of wild mint is as the main ingredient in a strong tea. Served steaming hot, wild mint tea helps dispel my daily cares and worries. But only recently did I start drinking this powerful beverage cold. One day I stopped into a little general store for some commercially made iced tea. One of its offerings was from a Native American tribe in Montana, who make their tea from wild mint gathered along the Bighorn River. Upon removing the cap I was amazed to find that this western mint was the same stuff I pick and enjoy here in New England. And, boy, did it quench my thirst.

Unfortunately the store closed, and as of yet no one else in my area carries that same brand of mint tea. But that's okay, since I can now make it myself. So can you.

Trees

The largest plants on the planet, trees furnish us with fruit, nuts, and lumber to build our homes. And yet foragers often fail to regard trees as proper objects of their avocation.

Trees offer many products that can be harvested year-round. That sets them head and shoulders (or perhaps crown and branch) above most other useful plants. Here are some examples.

The list of medicines derived from trees is practically endless. Red spruce roots were once used to sew birch bark together to make containers, baskets, and even canoes. Some trees can be worked into splints, which are used as weavers for baskets and even chair backs and seats. Cedar oil was once harvested commercially. The winged seeds of maple trees are edible and nutlike, and in a pinch the inner bark of many trees can be used as an emergency food.

WHITE PINE
Pinus strobus

Use: Tea
Range: Throughout New England
Similarity to toxic species: None
Best time: Year-round
Status: Common
Tools needed: None

Trees are not the first item that comes to mind when considering wild foods. And yet the stately white pine is the source of a healthful and, to my taste, pleasant tea.

The white pine is the official tree of the state of Maine, which has a long maritime history. White pine provided the straight, tall masts for the old sailing ships. In fact, because of a scarcity of ship's masts in the old country, in 1691 the British Crown declared that all white pine trees of at least 24 inches in diameter standing within 3 miles of the sea were the "King's Pines" and off-limits to colonists. The king might as well have told those independent New Englanders that they could no longer shoot bears, catch codfish, or drink rum; the King's Pines continued to run through New England sawmills despite the dictate.

A healthful tea can be made from white pine needles, which are easy to gather: Simply pull them from the branches. To make the tea, finely chop enough of the green needles to fill a teacup about one-third full. Add boiling water and let steep; strain and enjoy. You can add honey or sugar to taste, but try the tea "neat" first.

White pine is a rich source of vitamin C and a good source of vitamin A. With such readily available sources of these useful vitamins growing all around us, it seems a shame to pay money for synthetic vitamins.

Young white pines have a fairly smooth gray-green bark. Older trees have thick, grayish bark, with considerable fissuring. The needles, really the tree's leaves, grow in clusters of five, making for easy identification. To help remember this, just remember that the first half of the white pine's name has five letters, as do the leaves. You can't go wrong.

EASTERN HEMLOCK
Tsuga canadensis

Use: Tea

Range: Throughout New England

Similarity to toxic species: American yew (*Taxus canadensis*) is a small (3 feet tall), commonly cultivated shrub with red berries. The berries contain a single, poisonous seed, and the foliage itself is toxic in certain stages. The needles of the yew resemble those of eastern hemlock, but the similarity ends there. Foragers should have no difficulty differentiating between the mighty eastern hemlock and the American yew.

Best time: Year-round

Status: Common

Tools needed: None

The typical image of an early New England woodsman was of a hearty individual who wore wool pants, a knit hat, and a red-and-black-checkered shirt. This rugged soul carried a double-bitted ax and had a small teakettle fastened to his belt. The teakettle was used for a cup of hemlock tea at noontime.

Did the old-timers know that hemlock-needle tea was rich in vitamin C and that it could help any number of ail-

ments if taken in quantity? More likely, they drank it because they liked it. And that's mostly why I drink it.

Mature eastern hemlocks stand between 50 and 70 feet tall. The flat needles measure about ⅓ inch and are attached by means of a short petiole. They are not at all stiff or prickly and are shorter toward the tip of the twig. The cones measure about ¾ inch and are attached by tiny, thin stems. The bark is rough, with lots of ridges, and ranges in color from dark gray to red ochre.

Anyone who spends much time in the North Woods knows that the snow is never as deep under a hemlock tree as in other parts of the woods. Perhaps the way the flat needles are arranged helps deflect the snow. Wildlife, especially deer, are aware of the sanctuary afforded by hemlock trees and are quick to take advantage of it.

RECIPE

To make hemlock tea, simply pull a handful of fresh needles from a green twig, place them in a cup, cover with boiling water, and let steep. Wouldn't it be nice to go into the woods on some cold winter day, build a campfire, and, as the old-timers used to say, "byle up a kittle" of hemlock tea? Sometimes it is possible to bring back the old days!

RED SPRUCE
Picea rubens

Use: Chewing gum
Range: Throughout New England
Similarity to toxic species: None
Best time: Anytime the sap is not frozen
Status: Common
Tools needed: Any knife with a heavy blade

One of my favorite hikes leads to a barren, rocky mountaintop overlooking Maine's Penobscot Bay. The trail runs gradually uphill for about 1 mile to a plateau. From there it becomes steep for the short climb to the summit. It's at this point that the aroma of red spruce envelops the hiker. It is virtually impossible to continue on without pausing to inhale the almost overpowering fragrance. Many of the trees here have scars where limbs have been broken during times of high wind. From these scars flows the resinous sap that eventually hardens into the product woods-wise folks know as spruce gum.

At one point a Maine company made and distributed spruce gum. The gum was rendered, and impurities such as moss and sticks were removed. Then it was fashioned into little round balls and coated with cornstarch before being packaged. It saddened me greatly when the last box of spruce gum left the shelves of our local stores. It helped to know that I could still go into the woods and get my own spruce gum.

There's not much to picking the gum. Look for the hardened resin around scars on the red spruce tree. Pry it off and, with a knife blade, scrape the outside to remove any debris. Then begin chewing. At first the gum is crystalline and shatters. But it soon acquires a certain elasticity, the same as commercially produced chewing gum. This delightful gum is impregnated with the fragrance of the spruce tree. This fragrance remains in the gum much longer than does the synthetically produced flavor of commercial chewing gum.

I sometimes purposely scar young spruce trees on my own woodlot. This ensures a constant supply of spruce gum. Such minor scarring does not harm the trees in the least.

The mature red spruce tree usually has irregularly shaped, reddish scales on the bark. The needles, or leaves, are about ½ inch long and are sharp and prickly. Red spruce trees can grow to 80 feet tall and attain a diameter of 2 feet. The cones are reddish brown, 1 to 2 inches long, and shiny. Look for red spruce on the north side of ridges and hills.

WILLOWS
(White Willow, *Salix alba;* Black Willow, *Salix nigra;* other species of willow)

Uses: Tea, pain reliever. Fast-growing shoots may be stuck in streamside banks to sprout later and provide shade for trout and other fish. Also used in basket weaving, to make emergency snowshoes, and as a dowsing rod to locate sources of underground water.
Range: Throughout New England
Similarity to toxic species: None
Best time: Year-round
Status: Common and abundant
Tools needed: Jackknife

As a child I remember being told that willow, any willow, was good for trout. If you cut branches in the spring and stuck them along the banks, in only a few years willows would spring up and provide shade for the resident trout—and insects living in the trees would fall into the water and provide food for the fish. I have a fond hope that some huge old willows now provide shade for trout, courtesy of my youthful diligence.

FORAGER NOTE: The same potentially unpleasant properties of aspirin are present in white willow bark. While a powerful pain reliever, willow bark tea can also cause painful stomach upset.

Another youthful memory is of my grandpa using a freshly cut willow branch as a dowsing rod. Grandpa found water with ease, and he taught me the skill. And not surprisingly, my favorite medium for a water-dowsing rod is willow. (A water dowsing rod is a forked stick that dowsers use to locate water. They hold the stick in both hands and walk about, waiting for the end of the stick to dive down, indicating a source of water.)

Once after reading an old book on woodcraft, I decided to make a set of snowshoes using only basic materials that I could forage. I chose willow because the branches bend easily without breaking. These were not the best snowshoes, but I decided that had I been in the deep woods and needed to get out, the homemade snowshoes would have sufficed.

FORAGER NOTE: Maine's Penobscot Indians used small, dried chips of willow in their smoking mixtures. The willow turns to charcoal and glows for a long time, keeping the other ingredients lit. No doubt the smoke contains some of the willow's pain-relieving properties.

Still, it is the medicinal properties of willow that give this honorable tree a place in this volume. White willow (in my experience, most willows) contains salicin, an effective pain reliever and inflammation reducer. If the name of this naturally occurring acid sounds familiar, it is because acetylsalicylic acid was synthesized from salicin to make aspirin.

Willows are striking in their symmetry. In spring they are among the earliest trees to show some green. The willow's other uses are only icing on an already desirable cake.

Remedy: *To make willow tea, use a sharp jackknife to whittle about one-half teaspoon of the outer and inner bark; chop as finely as possible. Place in a cup, fill with boiling water, and let steep. Strain, if you prefer. Drink when cool. This is a powerful drug and will relieve all but the most obstinate pain symptoms.*

AMERICAN MOUNTAIN ASH
Sorbus americana

Synonym: Roundwood
Use: Jelly
Range: Throughout New England
Similarity to toxic species: None
Best time: September and October
Status: Common
Tools needed: None

The American mountain ash seems steeped in paradox. This tree sometimes reaches 40 feet in height but more often reaches only 20 feet, in which case it could be classified as a shrub. American mountain ash has alternate, finely toothed, compound leaves. These run between 13 and 17 inches long and are tapered at the end.

Despite its similarity to the white ash of New England, American mountain ash is not a true ash but rather a close relative of apple trees. But rather than bearing something akin to apples, this tree yields fruit that more closely resembles berries. These are bright orange, sometimes tending toward red.

To complicate identification even more, several other mountain ash trees have a similar appearance. Showy mountain ash (*S. decora*) grows in far northern New England. It has alternate compound leaves no more than 3 inches long. Showy mountain ash bears similar fruit, but the fruit is somewhat larger than that of American mountain ash. European mountain ash (*S. aucuparia*), also known as rowan tree, has leaves that are similar to American mountain ash, but the tree bears more and larger fruit.

The most common of these ashes is American mountain ash, but the berries of any of the mountain ash trees have similar uses. From here on out, this entry

RECIPE

The berries make a fine jelly. The recipe I offer here uses both mountain ash berries and apples. This combination makes a finer jelly than if either of these fruits were used singly. Note that this recipe does not call for added pectin, since mountain ash berries have an ample natural supply.

Gather three pounds of mountain ash berries and one pound of apples. Wash the berries and pull off the berry stalks, then wash the apples and cut them into small chunks, discarding the core. Put both berries and cut-up apples in a large saucepan and cover with water. Turn on the heat and simmer for forty-five minutes. Allow to cool, then strain through muslin or a jelly cloth. This is best done by making a bag of the fruit-filled cloth, tying it up with a string or cord, and hanging it over a large saucepan, allowing the liquid to drain out over time.

For each pint of liquid rendered, add one pound of granulated sugar. Bring to a boil, stirring until the sugar dissolves. Return to a simmer and continue heating until the liquid sets, which usually takes about thirty minutes. The solution has reached the setting point when a drop of liquid becomes firm when dropped on a cold plate. Skim any impurities from the surface of the liquid, then pour into sterilized jelly jars and seal the jars.

will refer to American mountain ash, since it has the widest distribution and is the one that most readers are most likely to encounter.

In my lifetime American mountain ash has become a favorite of municipal tree planters. So many of our New England villages, towns, and cities were once blessed with row upon row of stately American elm

FORAGER NOTE: I find mountain ash berries to be far too sour to be eaten raw, even after repeated frosts shrink the clinging berries and increase their sugar content.

trees. But with some rare exceptions, these have long since departed, victims of an imported disease. In an effort to find a substitute, planners frequently choose American mountain ash.

🌿 Remedy: *Besides making a superior jelly, mountain ash berries have a history of medicinal uses. The list of ills said to be cured by a tea made of the ripe fruit is long and, in my estimation, fanciful. One use, however, has merit. The astringent berries would probably be of some use where an astringent remedy is needed. This could include use as a gargle for a sore throat, mouth, or gums and as a rub for minor abrasions.*

WILD APPLE
Malus spp.

Synonym: Apple
Use: Raw fruit, dried, baked, ingredient in many different recipes
Range: Throughout New England
Similarity to toxic species: Wild crabapples may remotely resemble hawthorn (*Crataegus laevigata*), a plant with berries that are used to regulate heart function, something best done under the supervision of a physician.
Best time: October and November
Status: Locally abundant, widespread
Tools needed: None

Anyone coming upon a wild apple tree loaded with ripe fruit surely must wonder what species or type of apple it is. The answer: A wild apple is simply a wild apple.

Early colonists introduced apples to America, and these quickly became established residents, spreading far and wide through seed transferal by animals and birds. Consequently the progeny of the early varieties became many generations removed from the parent in taste and other important properties. Some, however, were noticeably different from the run-of-the-mill wild varieties. Many of these were selected for propagation and soon became named varieties, some of which have persisted into the present day.

To many foragers the location of a truly sweet and tasty wild apple tree is something to treasure and protect. Far too many wild trees produce small, hard, sour fruit. The only way to tell is to take a bite and judge from that.

Very often wild apples become quite a bit sweeter later in the season, after being hit with several hard frosts. Some even withstand prolonged freezing, only to grow even sweeter.

> FORAGER NOTE: How do we differentiate between truly wild apples and cultivated trees that have been abandoned and neglected? If you encounter a number of apple trees growing in close proximity, even in the middle of the woods, they were probably planted. But if a tree appears by itself, with no sign of human habitation such as a cellar hole, well, and so on nearby, it is probably a truly wild tree.

As an old-time bird hunter in the state of Maine back in the days when reverting farmland abounded and posted signs were rarely seen, I was fortunate to partake of the best of what nature offered. In October this meant woodcock, grouse, wild mushrooms, and wild apples. At the end of most days, the game pocket on my canvas hunting coat was packed with not only upland game but also lots of delicious wild apples. For me, most of the delight of wild apples was picking a mostly unblemished fruit from a tree, wiping it on my sleeve, and eating it right there and then.

Many people eschew wild apples because they look, well, unkempt. Wild apples often appear somewhat misshapen, with various little blemishes marking the skin. These things are usually sufficient to keep someone used to commercially produced apples away from the wild fruit. For me, these same traits are hallmarks of goodness. Wild trees are never sprayed with pesticide. And so what

RECIPE

Nothing beats wild apples for making applesauce. Simply peel the apples and discard skin, core, seeds, and stem, then cut them up into small pieces. Place in a medium saucepan with just a slight bit of water; set heat to medium-low. Add sugar to taste (for me, that's only two or three tablespoons per medium saucepan), stirring frequently until the apples soften. Mash with a potato masher if a smoother sauce is desired. Serve hot with a few sprinkles of ground cinnamon.

if an apple has a few little brown marks? Just take out your jackknife and remove the offending blemishes.

New England's plentiful and uncompromised wild apples represent a real treasure. Once you've located a tree with acceptable-tasting apples, bring a bag or basket home, and in addition to eating out of hand, use them in any pie recipe.

DRYING

Slice wild apples into thin rounds, and with a large-eyed needle, thread them on a string. Suspend them out of sunlight in a warm place to dry.

Wild crabapples are too sour for eating fresh but go well in any jelly recipe. If mountain ash berries are available, try the apple–ash berry jelly recipe in the entry on mountain ash.

Medicinal Plants

Plant medicines are as old as humankind. A decline in the use of plant medicines beginning in the early twentieth century has somewhat reversed itself thanks to the current wave of interest in all things natural. The popularity of alternative medicine has had a positive influence as well.

Commercial interests have jumped upon the "natural" bandwagon, and patented mixtures of common and not-so-common plants now are peddled on television and radio, in magazines, and in health food stores and supermarkets around the country. As someone raised by people who used indigenous medicinal plants as a matter of course, I find it amusing to see processed herbal remedies sold at such high prices.

High on my list of "things not to do" is buying herbal medicines, especially those that include foreign herbs with names I cannot pronounce. It makes no sense to me to shun modern medical care in favor of what I view as flimflammery. This is not to say that plant medicines are ineffective. Lots of plants common to New England provide highly effective remedies for a variety of ailments. Best of all, they are free.

In this chapter I describe my favorite medicinal plants. These are the ones I seek each year. This replenishment is necessary because the active shelf life of most herbs is only about one year.

Three of the more common methods of preparing plant matter for medicinal use are infusions, decoctions, and tinctures, or extracts.

Infusions are the quickest and easiest to prepare. An infusion is nothing more than a tea made from different plant parts. The general rule of measurement for infusions is one cup of boiling water poured over one teaspoon of dried plant matter or two teaspoons of chopped fresh plant matter. It is a good idea to begin with these suggested measurements and increase or decrease the plant-to-water ratio as needed. Flowers and leaves are best for infusions.

Decoctions are made by simmering plant material in water. This must be done only in a stainless-steel, glass, or enameled metal container. Other kinds of containers may react adversely with the plants. Decoctions are mostly used for the coarser plant parts such as bark, roots, and stems. The ratio of plant to water need not be as precise as in infusions; simply cover the chopped plant matter with water and simmer for thirty minutes. Above all, do not allow the water to boil. Let the mixture cool, and strain. Keep the unused portion in the refrigerator.

Tinctures, also called extracts, are the most time-consuming to produce, but plants preserved in this manner remain effective practically indefinitely. To make a tincture, soak plant matter in brandy or vodka. Some herb devotees insist on only "organic" vodka. Whether the potatoes or grain used to make the vodka was organically grown or not is of no consequence; the distilling process removes impurities. Besides, organic vodka costs much more than the conventional product. In my experience cheap vodka works just as well as the high-priced stuff.

Basic measurements for making tinctures are four ounces of dried (eight ounces of fresh) plant matter to one pint of alcohol. Cover the plant matter with the alcohol, and let the mixture sit in a dark, cool place for at least a couple of weeks. Strain the mixture through clean muslin into dark-colored bottles.

Some people feel that tinctures made according to the lunar cycle are more effective. For those inclined to add a bit of mysticism to their lives, here is the formula: Using the preceding instructions, make the tincture on a new moon and pour off, or strain, on a full moon.

Medicinal plants can interact, often with undesirable results, with prescription drugs. For that reason it is unwise to self-medicate with wild medicinal plants without first ascertaining whether that plant may do more harm than good. The easiest way is to check with a health-care professional about any potential drug interaction. The website www.naturaldatabase.com serves as a kind of online physician's desk reference regarding possible drug interactions as well as other warnings about using medicinal plants. The company does charge a fee, but this is on a sliding scale based on the length of time you want to sign up.

VALERIAN
Valeriana officinalis

Synonym: Garden heliotrope
Uses: Tranquilizer, sleep aid
Range: Throughout New England
Similarity to toxic species: The white flower clusters may be confused with some toxic members of the parsley family. Sniffing the bruised root will confirm whether or not the subject is valerian.
Best time: September through November
Status: Common and abundant
Tools needed: A spading fork or handheld trowel is usually needed to dig the roots.

Valerian is another example of how people will pay for something that they can easily gather themselves, for free.

Valerian is a powerful, natural tranquilizer and sleep aid. The root is gathered from fields, waste areas, and rural roadsides in late summer and early fall. The cleaned, dried, and chopped root is used in infusions for its calming effect and to help bring on sleep. A stronger product can be made by using the chopped root in a decoction.

Some herbal remedies work best when taken regularly, over a period of time. Valerian is the opposite—it works within minutes, with no known adverse side effects. There is a catch, however: Valerian root emits a powerful odor that some liken to old, dirty sweat socks. Interestingly, when in full bloom, valerian flowers emit a pleasant, sweet aroma, not at all like that of the roots. This alluring scent is most noticeable at night, when it fills the still summer air, charming all who pass by.

Valerian plants growing in poor, gravelly soil are generally more potent than those taken from rich, fertile soil.

Some years back I neglected to go to my favorite waste places to gather my winter's supply of valerian. Fortunately (I thought)

FORAGER NOTE: Valerian root is said to be what the Pied Piper of Hamelin used to charm the rats. I used valerian root as bait in mouse and rat traps and caught exactly nothing. Perhaps my local rodents have more sophisticated taste and will only visit traps baited with cheese or peanut butter. Valerian root may not charm rodents, but it does soothe weary, jittery people. And that is good enough reason to dig some next fall, dry it, and store it against a time of need.

I had used valerian in the back of a perennial flower bed as a foil for shorter plants. The roots were huge and, judging from the smell, would be plenty strong. Later that winter I turned to my store of valerian for help with insomnia. I made a strong tea, drank it, and returned to bed, certain the valerian would soon work its magic. It did not. I may as well have drunk caffeinated black tea for all the good my garden valerian did me.

Later I experimented by comparing valerian root dug from the rough gravel soil of rural Maine roadsides with valerian I had purposely cultivated and fed lots of good, rich compost. The wild stuff worked as expected, while the cultivated roots had virtually no effect whatsoever.

Valerian leaves are fernlike, divided, and roughly toothed. The flowers, which are borne in clusters on the top of the stalk, are pure white early on but acquire a pinkish hue later in the season.

SARSAPARILLA
Aralia nudicaulis

Use: Tonic
Range: Throughout New England
Similarity to toxic species: None
Best time: May through September
Status: Common and abundant
Tools needed: None

One of my favorite hobbies is collecting old-time medicine bottles. And one of my favorite bottles is a tall blue-green beauty with the embossed legend HOODS COMPOUND EXTRACT SARSAPARILLA. In the heyday of patent medicines, countless companies produced some kind of sarsaparilla extract or tonic. The lowly sarsaparilla was reputed to cure a host of complaints. Today people like me use it as a general tonic. It tastes good—and if some medicinal benefit can be attributed to taking it, so much the better.

Ironically, more people are familiar with wild sarsaparilla because of what it isn't rather than what it is. A member of the ginseng family, wild sarsaparilla closely resembles true ginseng and is frequently confused with that plant. If somebody were to give me a dollar for every time an excited forager showed me the "ginseng" he found, my bank account would swell considerably. Sarsaparilla root is similar to ginseng in that both have ridges on top. And, like ginseng, sarsaparilla root tends to branch, often resembling the human figure. But where true ginseng leaves are divided palmately—that is, the leafstalks are joined— sarsaparilla leaves are twice divided, with the bottom two leaves joining the stem some distance below the top set of three. Wild sarsaparilla has tiny white flowers, arranged in a globular shape atop a long stem. The dark blue berries appear soon after the flowers. Ginseng berries are red.

Sarsaparilla roots are exceedingly long, running in vast networks through the loose forest loam. Since wild sarsaparilla prefers the mottled shade of mixed-growth woods and the soil there is usually loose, no tools are needed to harvest the root. Simply grab the bottom of a sarsaparilla plant and gently pull, freeing the root with your other hand as it slips free of the earth.

Sarsaparilla root has a familiar, reassuring fragrance. It reminds me of an old-time general store. Its good taste and pleasing aroma make sarsaparilla a pleasant medicine to take. Try it when that run-down feeling strikes.

YARROW
Achillea millefolium

Synonyms: Thousand-leaf, woundwort
Uses: Cold, flu, and fever remedy; styptic; toothache remedy; tonic
Range: Throughout New England
Similarity to toxic species: None
Best time: June through October
Status: Common and abundant
Tools needed: None

While nothing cures a cold, some plants, including yarrow, can alleviate the symptoms. An old-time formula for a botanical cold and fever medicine consists of equal parts of yarrow, elderberry blossoms, and peppermint. Yarrow also can be used alone in an infusion for colds, flus, and fevers.

Yarrow is a fairly effective plant medicine. The leaves can be chewed to relieve a toothache. They can also be ground, crushed, or slightly chewed and applied directly to minor cuts as a styptic.

The common wild yarrow, with its creamy white blossoms, is an alien plant, probably brought here purposely for medicinal use. It has since escaped cultivation and is common nearly everywhere. Other forms of yarrow, some in strikingly attractive colors, are cultivated as plants for the perennial flower bed. So while wild yarrow is ruthlessly pulled and hoed as a weed, its more colorful brethren are admired and pampered.

Pick yarrow while the plant is in flower, and dry and store in a dark, cool spot. Use the dried leaves and flowers in an infusion. If taken hot, two ounces at a time, it can induce sweating. Lesser amounts, taken cold, have a tonic effect.

Yarrow can grow to 3 feet high. Its distinctive, soft, fernlike leaves clasp the stem. The tiny flowers are borne in dense clusters, atop the stem. Look in waste places, on roadsides, along dirt or gravel drives, and in old abandoned fields. Yarrow is at home in city lots as well as country dooryards, making it available to just about everyone.

BONESET
Eupatorium perfoliatum

Synonym: Thoroughwort
Uses: Fever reducer, laxative
Range: Throughout New England
Similarity to toxic species: None
Best time: July and August
Status: Common
Tools needed: None

"I know what that is," said an elderly participant at one of my slide presentations. "That's thoroughwort. Father used to take us kids out every year and gather all we could find. When we got home, he made us drink as much of it as we could stand. He did this with one child, one day at a time. We had an outhouse, and whoever took the thoroughwort would spend most of the day there. It cleaned us out real good!"

Boneset, or thoroughwort, is also as good a medicine for fever as any over-the-counter medicine you might buy in the store. Additionally, boneset is accorded a number of other attributes, reportedly once used to treat malaria, rheumatism, muscular pains, spasms, pneumonia, pleurisy, and gout.

Even if boneset had no other redeeming qualities, its physical appearance alone would be sufficient cause for appreciation. Growing as high as 5 feet, boneset presents a striking picture, with its flat clusters of white flowers atop a stem that apparently grows through its alternating, twinned leaves. If boneset were not so common, it would surely be prized as a specimen plant by flower gardeners.

Pick boneset leaves just as the plant goes into flower. The flowers too are medicinally active and can be added to the leaves. Look in wet areas, along roadside ditches, in moist woods, and along swamps and bogs. The drainage ditch along my driveway is home to lots of boneset, as well as skullcap, jewelweed, and several other useful medicine plants, so it's easy for me to determine just when my local boneset is ready for picking.

The common name boneset stems from the plant's use in treating outbreaks of what was called breakbone (Dengue) fever. Apparently victims of that disease were so tortured by pain that they assumed horribly contorted positions, causing some to worry that the victims would break their bones.

Use boneset in an infusion at the first sign of a fever. It has a bitter taste, which appeals to me. Others may want to add sweetener.

And for those gardeners who dare to be different, why not transplant a young boneset plant to a shady, damp section of the flower bed? Perhaps you will start a new fad!

HEAL-ALL
Prunella vulgaris

Synonyms: Self-heal, bumblebee weed
Uses: Sore throat remedy, diarrhea remedy
Range: Throughout New England
Similarity to toxic species: None
Best time: July through October
Status: Common and abundant
Tools needed: None

My earliest memory of being treated with wild medicinal plants is when I was seven years old. I had a fever coupled with severe diarrhea. The family doctor paid a house call (that should help date the incident) and gave me something that eventually helped the fever but had no effect on the diarrhea, which continued for days afterward. I remember my mother being terribly worried about my weight loss. She called my grandpa and asked if he knew of any plant remedy that might save his grandson. That afternoon Grandpa came to the house, a bunch of weeds in hand. He brewed up a terrible-tasting concoction and made me drink it by the waterglass. It stopped the diarrhea cold. Now I harvest heal-all each fall and dry and store it for winter use.

Heal-all—or bumblebee weed, as Grandpa's generation called it (the flowers attract bumblebees)—is an unscented member of the mint family. Only its square stem betrays its lineage. Heal-all grows in semishade along wooded lanes, driveways, and the edges of fields and woodland openings.

Heal-all should be gathered when in flower and dried for year-round use. Note that the flower spike is never completely covered with blossoms; instead, half a dozen blossoms at a time may open, giving the plant an unfinished appearance. The paired, ovate leaves have few if any teeth and grow opposite each other on the branched stem. Heal-all can grow to about 1 foot high but more often reaches only 5 or 6 inches.

The point of gathering heal-all or any other medicinal plant is to have the plants on hand if they are needed. Gathering and processing the plants is hands-on work in nature—something to look forward to each year. In time, even if you never use the plants medicinally, they become old, familiar friends, cheering us and adding to our contentment. And that to me is the most valuable aspect of medicinal plants.

Remedy: *Heal-all can be made into a tea, or infusion, for use as a gargle for a sore throat. I prefer to simmer the whole plant—leaves, blossoms, and stems—in a decoction until at least half the water has evaporated. The resulting dark liquid can be allowed to cool and gargled to good effect. Also, the stronger decoction is more effective as a diarrhea remedy. Take two ounces at a time, every hour or so, as needed.*

COMMON SAINT-JOHN'S-WORT
Hypericum perforatum

Use: Medicinal tea, taken for depression
Range: Throughout New England
Similarity to toxic species: None
Best time: August and September
Status: Common and abundant
Tools needed: None

Each fall my neighbor walks the edges of his fields and farm lanes, searching for his winter supply of medicinal plants. One of his favorites is Saint-John's-wort (also called St. Johnswort). "I take a cup of it on dark days and it cheers me up," he told me. Both the blossoms and the leaves are included in his brew. That this man is cheered from his occasional Saint-John's-wort tea cannot be disputed. But since Saint-John's-wort, among other herbs, has a cumulative effect and must be taken over a long period of time to be effective, how can a single cup of tea cheer anyone? Moreover, because most recipes call for the flowers only, my neighbor's tea may be weaker than if he used only the blossoms. What gives here?

First, consider when Saint-John's-wort is ready for picking. It is at its peak in late summer and early fall—that glorious New

England mini season that encompasses the best of two worlds: bright, balmy days and cool, crisp nights. A more cheerful time of year cannot be imagined. Second, picking medicinal plants is just plain fun. Third, it's reassuring to know that in a single day it's possible to harvest a season's supply of beneficial plants. In short, everything about the medicinal plant harvest is positive and upbeat. Drinking a cup of Saint-John's-wort tea revives all these pleasant thoughts. So now it's easy to understand how my neighbor is cheered every time he downs a cup of tea.

Saint-John's-wort is not only a useful medicinal plant but also a pretty wildflower with some attractive characteristics. The botanical name for its species, *perforatum,* discloses an interesting physical property: The leaves are dotted with little round holes. Lacking very young eyes, it is necessary to use a handheld magnifier to fully appreciate these holes or, more accurately, oil pockets. I think the pockets look much like moon-style craters, with a small berm on the surface.

Saint-John's-wort leaves are paddle shaped and opposite, small in comparison to the size of the plant. The bright yellow flowers have five petals with bristly stamens. Although the plant can grow to about 18 inches tall, it can also be recumbent. There is one such vining specimen in the rock garden in front of my cottage.

Saint-John's-wort, along with purple coneflower (*Echinacea purpurea*), has made untold millions of dollars for various companies, each claiming that its product is superior to other over-the-counter herbal remedies. Their logic is that the commercial product is somehow controlled into a standard strength. Someone once told me that it would be impossible to get the same benefit from wild Saint-John's-wort as from the commercial product. In response I can say only that the Greeks had a word for such nonsense—baloney! All right, maybe it wasn't the Greeks, but the point is that Saint-John's-wort is Saint-John's-wort, no matter how you slice it. Here's my advice for those who don't want to spend a small fortune for the commercially available stuff.

Remedy: *Pick the plant in blossom. Try to get more flowers than leaves, but don't worry about the ratio of each, as long as the stems are discarded. Dry the plant in a shady, cool, and airy location. When dry, rub it between your palms; store it in a closed jar or bag. Use a teaspoon to make a cup of tea to cheer the spirits.*

Herbalists will recommend that the tea be taken daily for the relief of depression. I cannot say if this works or not, since I've never been truly depressed. But the occasional cup is enough to lift my spirits, and many experts say that regular use of Saint-John's-wort does combat true depression.

CANADA GOLDENROD
Solidago canadensis

Synonyms: Goldenrod, solidago
Uses: Leaf tea for fever and gas; blossoms chewed for sore throat
Range: Throughout New England
Similarity to toxic species: None
Best time: August and September
Status: Common and widespread; despised weed
Tools needed: None

Canada goldenrod is widespread throughout the Northeast and is easily distinguished from other goldenrod species by the leaves. They are sharply toothed and have a prominent center vein with two parallel, curved outer veins. The bright yellow blossoms are borne on horizontal plumes, with the exception of the very tip, which is more or less a continuation of the main stalk of the plant.

Once blooming goldenrod saddened me because it signaled the end of summer. That was before I recognized that blooming plants represent separate seasons, special times on nature's calendar. Goldenrod, for instance, blooms at the same time as Saint-John's-wort, butter-and-eggs, sow thistles, and a host of other wild plants having yellow blossoms. Indeed, because so many plants with yellow blossoms are at their peak now, this might rightly be called "the yellow season."

At least that's how I define it. The yellow season should be appreciated for what it is—a short but glorious page on the grand list of annual events.

Watery eyes, runny noses, hacking and wheezing—allergy season happens every fall. Most allergy sufferers blame goldenrod for these unpleasant symptoms. But while goldenrod can cause allergic reactions in some individuals, the bulk of allergy sufferers are victims of ragweed, not goldenrod, pollen.

Because goldenrod gets such bad press, I make an example of it as a "good weed"—a beautiful and useful, if largely unappreciated, plant. When the Canada goldenrod (the most common species in our area) comes into bloom, I pick the most symmetrically shaped blooming ends and put them in a vase, along with some orange hawkweed for contrast. And because the goldenrods bloom so late in the year, it is possible to add them to bouquets of blue- and magenta-colored New England asters. Such visually appealing combinations of color and style are hallmarks of late summer in New England.

Given that Canada goldenrod has far more benefits than detriments, it is time for foragers to become patrons of this handsome yet maligned plant of the fields, hedgerows, and waste places.

Remedy: *Goldenrod leaf tea is a pleasant beverage, but more than that, an infusion of leaves and blossoms can dispel stomach gas. It also encourages sweating, which can help alleviate fever symptoms. Use one tablespoon dried or two tablespoons fresh herb to one cup boiling water.*

Remedy: *Even people who aren't sensitive to ragweed pollen can experience some discomfort during the allergy season. Fortunately Canada goldenrod is ready to step into the gap, especially when a scratchy or sore throat makes life miserable. When I have a sore throat, I chew on fresh blossoms of Canada goldenrod. The pleasantly spicy taste alone would be reason enough to partake, but the fact is, the stuff alleviates minor sore throat discomfort. Just pick and chew—so simple yet so effective.*

GOLDTHREAD
Coptis groenlandica

Synonym: Canker root
Uses: An appetite-stimulating tonic; a tincture gargled for mouth sores or sore throat; a tea used for colds; a root chewed for canker sores
Range: Throughout New England
Similarity to toxic species: None
Best time: Whenever the ground is not frozen
Status: Common and abundant
Tools needed: None

Goldthread grows in lush colonies on the forest floor, thriving in the partial shade and cool, damp conditions afforded by a mixed-growth canopy. Goldthread is also common in sphagnum bogs. As with so many common woodland plants, almost everybody has seen goldthread, but few have ever taken time to examine it carefully. Fewer still can accurately identify the plant.

As the common name implies, the roots of goldthread are long, thin, and a bright yellow color. Each goldthread plant has a great mass of roots, most of which grow laterally only an inch or two beneath the surface. The shiny evergreen leaves have coarse teeth and grow in groups of three, much like strawberry leaves. The pretty white flowers have five sepals and five petals.

Harvesting goldthread roots is a cinch. Goldthread always grows on loose ground, and all the forager needs to do is lift the top layer of forest litter or sphagnum moss with bare fingers to expose the vast network of brilliant yellow roots. Picking the individual roots is somewhat tedious, but ten minutes of effort can produce a great quantity.

The easiest way to use goldthread is to pick a root, brush it clean, and chew on it. This applies the medicine directly to the mouth and is an efficient way to treat any sores of the mouth or gums. The next, and perhaps most interesting, way to use goldthread root is as a bitter tonic. The reasons for taking bitters are given in the entry on ground ivy (see page 199) and needn't be repeated here, except to say that if you appreciate the bitter digestive tonic made from ground ivy, you will probably enjoy the goldthread product even more. It has a clean, sharp taste, one I find both pleasant and stimulating.

Given goldthread's effectiveness as a medicine, its virtues as a digestive aid, and its abundance and easy availability, it should rank high on every forager's list of medicinal plants.

Remedy: *To make goldthread tonic, chop the fresh roots finely, using one teaspoon chopped root to one cup of boiling water. These proportions may be modified according to taste. Let the mixture steep for thirty minutes before straining. Use one teaspoon of the tonic before meals to aid in digestion. It can also be used as a gargle for sore throats and hoarseness. Refrigerate unused portions.*

Remedy: *Make a tincture of goldthread for use in winter, when the ground is frozen and the fresh root cannot be obtained. A goldthread tincture is one of the more effective and reliable sore throat medicines. Besides using it myself, I have given this product to ailing friends; without exception, they have gained some amount of relief. Use four ounces of dried or eight ounces of fresh goldthread to one pint of alcohol, vodka being preferred. Cover the plant matter with alcohol. Let the mixture sit in a dark, cool place for at least a couple of weeks, then strain through clean muslin into dark-colored bottles.*

SPOTTED JOE-PYE WEED
Eupatorium maculatum

Synonym: Smokeweed
Use: The leaf tea as a cold and flu remedy
Range: Throughout New England
Similarity to toxic species: None
Best time: August
Status: Common and abundant
Tools needed: None

"It won't be long now. The joe-pye weed is already blooming," a friend once told me. His observation was really a comment that the summer was fast drawing to a close. Joe-pye weed blooms in August, a prelude to the approaching autumn.

Abundant in northern New England, joe-pye weed grows to about 4 feet tall. The cupped, lance-shaped leaves are coarsely toothed and surround the stem in whorls of four or five leaves each. The flower clusters are borne atop the plant and are pink to red in color. Spotted joe-pye weed prefers damp ground, growing in roadside ditches and along streamsides. Several other joe-pye weeds are found in New England, including sweet joe-pye weed (*E. purpureum*), so named because the crushed flowers emit a vanilla-like scent), and joe-pye weed (*E. dubium*). Both species are more common in southern New England.

Spotted joe-pye weed is a striking plant, used by innovative gardeners as a background plant in perennial beds. Medicinally, the various joe-pye weeds are similar in action to boneset. I use the two interchangeably. Traditionally it is the roots that are used medicinally, but I use the leaves in an infusion and find they work just fine.

Although a host of other medicinal claims are made for spotted joe-pye weed, I prefer to use it only for the common cold, flu, and fever.

MUGWORT
Artemisia vulgaris

Uses: Poultice of leaves for rheumatism; steeped as a tea for a digestive tonic and for cold and fever relief
Range: Throughout New England
Similarity to toxic species: Mugwort closely resembles wormwood (*A. absinthium*), which contains thujone, a toxin.
Best time: August and September
Status: Common and abundant
Tools needed: None

The person who coined the term *weed* must have been thinking of mugwort. It is virtually everywhere. Present in every vacant lot, railroad siding, landfill, and waste area, mugwort is familiar to anyone who has ever stepped outside. Even in the early season, mugwort looks half dead and scruffy because the bottom leaves dry, curl, turn yellow, and then brown. Who would ever guess this unassuming, omnipresent weed has considerable medicinal value?

Mugwort leaves are deeply cut, light green on top, and silver colored on the bottom. When a stiff wind turns the leaves up, the plant assumes a ghostly shade of silver. The tiny, fuzzy, yellowish-brown "flowers" grow in bunches at the end of the stem. The crushed leaves and flowers emit a pungent aroma.

Mugwort is another plant with a plethora of virtues attached to it. One herbal guide describes it as helpful in cases of rheumatism, gout, kidney and bladder trouble, female trouble (whatever that may be), and suppressed menstruation. This same booklet fails to indicate mugwort's use as a digestive tonic or its use against the common cold and accompanying fever. However, the latter two uses are the only ones I can personally recommend.

The way to pick mugwort is to slide your hand along the stem, pulling bunches of leaves. There is no need to break the stem.

DRYING

Dried mugwort leaves are handy to have in the medicine cabinet during fall and winter, the cold and flu season. To dry, spread mugwort leaves loosely on a nylon screen nailed to a wooden frame and hang the frame with the leaves in a cool, dark place until the leaves are totally dry and crumbly. Then place in an airtight container.

RECIPE

An aromatic cup of mugwort tea tickles the senses, warms the soul, and fights cold symptoms all at the same time. To make a cup of mugwort tea, place either one tablespoon dried or two tablespoons fresh leaves in a cup and fill the cup with boiling water. The leaves will settle to the bottom, but go ahead and strain if desired.

MOTHERWORT
Leonurus cardiaca

Synonyms: The Japanese consider their species of motherwort an "herb of life."
Use: Medicinal tea
Range: Throughout New England
Similarity to toxic species: None
Best time: August and September
Status: Common and abundant
Tools needed: Motherwort is prickly; wear gloves when harvesting leaves.

Motherwort was one of those plants I studied in books but didn't see firsthand until about fifteen years ago. While camping I strolled from my tent down to a nearby stream, and there was a huge motherwort plant, which I recognized immediately from years of seeing it in photographs.

From that initial encounter, motherwort immediately went out of sight and out of mind. Then in summer 2011 a familiar-looking "weed" appeared near one of my garden beds. It was motherwort, no doubt brought in with a load of compost from a local dairy farm. This was enough to send me to my library to try to determine if any of its reputed healing properties would suit me. Among the long list of uses, motherwort tea was listed as treating sciatica and insomnia, both of which frequently plague me. So the day prior to the first frost, I picked a quantity of motherwort leaves and placed them loosely in a brown ash basket to dry. I later stored the leaves in a sealed glass container.

When I asked my doctor, a homeopath, for his opinion of motherwort, he told me to bring some of the herb along at my next visit, and he would determine if it was good for me or not. My doctor uses kinesiology (the scientific study of human movement) to determine how different substances affect the body, and he told me my body liked motherwort.

I cannot yet report much success in having motherwort cure any ills, but it often takes time for herbal medicines to work their magic.

I can tell you how the stuff tastes, though. My first impression upon sipping a cup of hot motherwort tea was that I was ingesting a mixture of licorice and hay. It had that kind of aroma. I found it slightly bitter at first, but not overly much. That bitterness became more pronounced after about twenty minutes. Motherwort has a lingering bitter, though not entirely unpleasant, aftertaste; in that respect, I liken it to skullcap.

The common name, motherwort, arises from the plant's use as a childbirth aid. Other ailments motherwort is said to cure include asthma, heart palpitations, fever, stomachache, nervousness, delirium, and muscle spasms. Several species are listed as having sedative effects.

One Maine family I know asserts that motherwort helps them feel better overall. Perhaps. At least I'm convinced it works for them.

To identify motherwort, look for a plant with a square stem (which places it in the mint family) and prickly leaves. These have three deeply cleft lobes, and each lobe terminates in a slender point. As with any mint, flowers grow in leaf axils. The young bud groups are also prickly. The plant grows up to 5 feet tall. The overall appearance of motherwort is so striking that once seen, it is never forgotten.

RECIPE

As with most leafy herbs, motherwort is often used as a tea, or infusion. Use the standard formula of one teaspoon dried herb to one cup boiling water. Let steep until the water turns dark; either sip immediately or remove the leaves by lifting out with a fork, allowing excess liquid to drip back into the cup before discarding the leaves.

The Waste Places

Lots of useful plants grow in waste places—areas where the ground is poor, wet, or perhaps a trifle too acidic, rocky, windy, or otherwise inhospitable to most cultivated plants. These spots are everywhere: behind someone's house in town, along the country dweller's driveway. They may include the unmowed edge of a community baseball field or the weedy bank where garden refuse and grass clippings are unceremoniously dumped.

No matter where they're found, waste places provide a unique habitat for dozens of edible and medicinal plants.

JAPANESE KNOTWEED
Polygonum cuspidatum

Synonym: Bamboo
Uses: Cooked vegetable, stewed vegetable, pie filling
Range: Throughout New England
Similarity to toxic species: None
Best time: April and May; into early June in the north
Status: Common; despised as an invasive weed
Tools needed: None

Most home owners who have knotweed growing on their property hate the stuff. Japanese knotweed is number one on lists of invasive plants. Countless hours of toil are wasted in trying to eradicate Japanese knotweed, and untold gallons of toxic poisons are introduced into the environment in a misplaced effort to kill the plant. Personally, I prefer to eat it. Knotweed is truly a food for the nonconformist.

Most people think Japanese knotweed is a form of bamboo. It is not. It's in the buckwheat family, related to another edible plant, lady's thumb. Knotweed is confused with bamboo because the stem has similar-looking nodes.

Japanese knotweed was introduced to this country in the Victorian era as an ornamental. It does have a rather attractive style, but the flowers, which were the main drawing card back then, are too small and their whitish-green color too drab to elicit much praise today. Since then knotweed has spread across the country, although never far from the original plantings. Search any old homestead or look around any old rock foundation and chances are two plants will be growing nearby: a huge, ancient lilac bush and a great stand of Japanese knotweed.

Knotweed grows to about 10 feet high. The olive-drab stems are smooth, shiny, and hollow. They are often mottled with red spots, as if somebody splashed paint on them. The node joints are covered with a papery membrane, much like knotweed's relative, lady's thumb. The leaves are wide, are roundly pointed, and lack teeth. The flowers, which bloom in late summer, are borne on long, thin stalks.

In spring, when the blackflies are at their gnawing, swarming worst, Japanese knotweed sends up its young shoots. This is the time to pick the stuff, before the plant grows higher than a few feet. The way to tell if a knotweed shoot is still tender, even if it is fairly tall, is to bend the very end. The last 6 or 8 inches should snap easily, with a hollow, popping sound. Two people picking at once make a sound like popcorn popping. Since knotweed grows in vast colonies (some more than a hundred years old), it's easy to snap off half a bushel in no time.

It is not necessary to remove the undeveloped leaves at the tip of the shoot, although any larger leaves growing from the sheaths on the nodes should be removed.

While Japanese knotweed is best harvested in mid- to late spring, it can be located at any time of the year. Look for the dried, brown, bamboo-like stalks from the previous year's crop.

Invite the neighbors—preferably neighbors who have spent their weekend digging and cursing the Japanese knotweed on the edge of their lawn—to dinner. Set out a nice spread, with wine, candles, and pretty appetizers before the meal. As the featured vegetable, serve steamed Japanese knotweed shoots, but don't tell your guests what it is. Only reveal the identity of this delicious "mystery" vegetable after the commensurate amount of pleading and prodding. Oh, the devious mind of the hard-core forager!

JEWELWEED
Impatiens capensis

Synonym: Spotted touch-me-not
Uses: Cooked green; poison ivy and rash remedy
Range: Throughout New England, especially in shady, moist places and on roadsides
Similarity to toxic species: None
Best time: April and May
Status: Common and abundant
Tools needed: None

Jewelweed is a crossover plant: It is eminently edible yet has great medicinal value. Jewelweed is among the earliest fresh green plants available in New England. In early spring, as soon as wood frogs begin their sporadic croaking in the wet areas, I search for jewelweed seedlings. These, although small, can be gathered in great handfuls. At this point it is the seed leaves, or cotyledons, along with the weak, succulent stalks that are eaten. A few weeks later the plant takes on something like its adult appearance, although it is still only 6 inches high.

Jewelweed is so called because water beads up on the "unwettable" leaves; when the sun hits them, the little droplets gleam like so many jewels. Sunrise on

Wash the immature jewelweed shoots in a colander and trim any roots that remain attached. Drop a few handfuls into a slight amount of boiling water, or cook in a vegetable steamer. Five minutes is more than enough time to cook the young jewelweed shoots. Drain and serve with a pat of butter, seasoned to taste.

The older plants, up to 12 inches tall, are edible too, but the stems become tough. At this point it is best to use only the leaves and tender tips. Cooking takes a bit longer as well.

a still, summer morning is my favorite time of day to poke about outside and watch the jewelweed glisten in the morning light.

The plants grow in dense colonies along country roads, ditches, and driveways. Interestingly, the ground under jewelweed plants is always moist, even on the hottest days of summer. The smooth, lightly ribbed leaves are more or less spear shaped; the succulent stems are partially translucent; and the orange, trumpet-shaped blossoms hang from a thin, flexible stem.

The ripe seedpods are pressure-sensitive and forcibly eject their cargo of seeds when touched. Children (including big kids like me) love squeezing the seedpods and watching the seeds, with their clock-spring-shaped triggers, spew forth. It's great fun to gently pick only the largest seedpods; when you've gathered a handful (this is hard to do without them bursting prematurely), touch one and watch it set off a chain reaction.

FREEZING

Jewelweed's curative powers can be preserved for off-season use too. Gather an armload of stems and leaves; simmer in a large saucepan, or a clam and lobster steamer, until the water is reduced by half and has turned a deep, dark brown. Lift out and discard the spent jewelweed, and allow the juice to cool. As soon as it's cool, pour the liquid into ice cube trays and freeze. After the cubes are frozen, remove them from the trays and put them in a plastic bag for immediate use at any time.

Though jewelweed is a superb vegetable, it is more widely known for its healing qualities. Indeed, many people who are familiar with the plant as a medicinal herb are surprised to learn that it is equally as useful on the table. Jewelweed is most useful as a curative when it is mature, or nearly so.

Remedy: *For the itch of poison ivy, just crush the juicy stems of jewelweed and rub on the affected area. For immediate protection when you unexpectedly encounter poison ivy in the field, rub on jewelweed. As long as the body part that touched the poison ivy is washed with soap and water later on, the rash probably won't develop.*

Poison ivy is not the only itch that jewelweed treats. The itch of heat rash, bug bites, and a host of other complaints are all nullified by a poultice of crushed jewelweed stems and leaves.

You also can drop a few of those frozen jewelweed cubes in the bathwater to help soothe itchy, dry skin. Or place a cube in a washcloth and gently wipe the itchy skin.

COMMON MILKWEED
Asclepias syriaca

Use: Several kinds of cooked vegetables

Range: Throughout New England

Similarity to toxic species: Butterfly weed (*A. tuberosa*) is a toxic member of the milkweed family. Butterfly weed has orange flowers, the stem does not exude a milky latex when broken (common milkweed does), and the seedpods are thinner than those of common milkweed. Although very young common milkweed shoots are edible, it is advisable not to pick them because of their similarity to young members of the toxic dogbane family, the genus *Apocynum*.

Best time: June for tender tips, July for blossoms and seedpods

Status: Common and abundant

Tools needed: Gloves protect the hands from the sticky, latex-like sap.

Milkweed leaves are nearly oblong, except they are roundly pointed at the tip. They grow opposite each other. All parts of the plant exude a sticky, milky substance when broken. The seedpods are 2 inches or longer, green, and warty.

FORAGER NOTE: The milky sap is toxic, but cooking destroys the toxins. Never consume the raw sap.

An old woman, a friend of the family, first enlightened me as to the edible qualities of common milkweed. When this lady was a youngster, her family relished the young milkweed tips, picking only the four-leaved top of the young plant. These they ate boiled, after the manner of string beans or cabbage. It took me only as long as the short drive to the nearest milkweed patch to sample this product. They were excellent.

People who would never dream of eating common milkweed still use it. The seedpods are routinely gathered and dried by those who make dried flower arrangements. Sometimes the warty pods are sprayed with gold enamel. And every child who witnesses the wind carrying the fluffy seeds from the opened seedpod feels compelled to help the process by gathering bunches of the seedpods and scattering their contents to the prevailing wind.

RECIPE

When the plant is young, the tips, with their four leaves, are edible. Here's what to look for: Looking down at the plant, you'll see two small leaves directly opposite each other and see two more leaves, this time smaller and again opposite each other, half a turn removed. The leaf configuration, then, will resemble a plus (+) sign.

Snip these leaves with thumb and forefinger. Steam for about fifteen minutes and serve with butter, salt, and pepper. Some people find common milkweed bitter to the taste and so cook it in two waters. Get the water boiling first. Thoroughly wash the leaves, then immerse them in the boiling water. Leave the leaves in the boiling water for at least twenty minutes, drain the leaves, and discard the water.

RECIPE

When the plant blossoms, the globular clusters of unopened flower buds offer yet another food product. These buds are good until the flowers begin to open. Although the flowers are tinged with lavender, they turn green when boiled for at least ten minutes. Change the water during cooking if desired to reduce any bitterness. These are so well liked by guests at my wild-food luncheons that I regularly freeze quantities of the clusters in order to ensure a steady supply, even out of season. The texture of the cooked buds somewhat resembles broccoli, although the taste is completely different.

EXTRA RECIPE

When young and firm, the seedpods make an unusual and delicious food. The cooked husk becomes soft and tender, and the silken seeds congeal. The texture and taste of the pods makes them a personal favorite of mine, and I always freeze some for winter use.

Cook the pods until tender; use two waters if desired.

GREAT BURDOCK
Arctium lappa

Synonym: Burdock
Use: Cooked vegetable
Range: Throughout New England
Similarity to toxic species: None
Best time: Young leaves in April and early May; stalks in June and July
Status: Common and abundant; despised as an invasive weed
Tools needed: None

Dog owners know all too well the difficulty of removing the burrs of great burdock and common burdock (*A. minus*) from their pet's coat. The burrs, which contain the plant's seeds, also pose a hazard for humans who wear wool shirts

RECIPE

The roots of the first-year plants (burdock is biennial) are edible. The work begins with digging the long taproots. (Note that they do not give up without a fight.) Peel the roots and cook in two waters for up to thirty minutes. Serve as a root vegetable. Burdock roots are relished in Japan.

or pants; the burrs' individual "hooks" can only be removed through tedious, painstaking effort.

Look on south-facing slopes of gravel banks and other rough, waste places for the first burdock leaves of the season. The mature plant somewhat resembles rhubarb, in that the leaves are roughly the same size. The round burrs are brown and prickly; the stalks of the basal leaves have a slight groove. The plant grows more than 8 feet high. Who would ever think this coarse plant was not only edible but tasty too?

Burdock provides several food products. First, and easiest to deal with, are the young leaves. These can be harvested in very early spring, as soon as the top layer of ground thaws. The leaves are egg shaped and extremely wavy, or crinkled, on the margins. When the leaves are from 2 to 3 inches long, they make a good boiling green.

RECIPE

Boil the leaves for at least fifteen minutes to render them tender. Some prefer to cook burdock leaves in two waters. I use only one but sometimes add a small pinch of baking soda to tenderize the leaves and to remove any inherent bitterness. Burdock leaves don't lose much bulk in cooking, so what you begin with is pretty much what you end with—a true Yankee bargain if ever there was one.

EXTRA RECIPE

The inner core of the young leafstalks and flower stalks is edible, either raw or cooked, but the process of removing the outside rind is tedious. Cook the cores in the same way as the roots.

ORPINE
Sedum purpureum

Synonym: Live-forever
Uses: Trail nibble, salad ingredient, cooked vegetable
Range: Throughout New England
Similarity to toxic species: None
Best time: April and May
Status: Common and abundant
Tools needed: A hand trowel helps dislodge the tubers.

Rural youngsters know this plant not for its culinary properties, but because it is fun to separate the edges of the fleshy leaves, blow on the seam, and make an ersatz balloon, which can later be popped between the palms.

Adults may see some similarity between a common rock garden plant, autumn joy sedum, and common orpine. The resemblance is more than superficial, since both belong to the same genus.

Orpine leaves are smooth and succulent; that is, fat and fleshy. They are light green, have smooth, rough teeth, and grow alternately on the stem in a whorl. The tuberous roots resemble thin parsnips and seldom reach more than 2 inches long.

The flavor of the young leaves is mild yet pronounced. Once while on an early-season fishing trip, the trout refused to bite. But the field that bounded the stream was filled with young orpine, the leaves at just the perfect stage for munching. I went home fishless but full from eating a huge quantity of orpine leaves.

Around the time the ostrich fern fiddleheads are ripe, which in my part of New England is around the first week of May, the orpine tubers are ready. The tubers are good as soon as they can be located in spring, but I like to combine fiddleheading with tuber picking. And although a trowel is sometimes needed to remove the abundant tubers from the ground, orpine's tendency to grow on gravel banks ensures that the ground is usually loose and the plant—roots, tubers, and all—can be uprooted without any mechanical assistance.

Each plant hosts a large bunch of elongated tubers. These grow laterally in the ground, with tubers branching out in all directions. Select the largest from each group, and return the rest to the soil to propagate another clump of orpine.

RECIPE

At home, rinse all sand and gravel from the tubers and boil for fifteen to twenty minutes. Serve with butter, salt, and pepper. These go nicely with a dish of boiled ostrich fern fiddleheads, supplying the "potato" part of the meal. A few fresh trout complement the feast nicely. For a finishing touch, serve a salad of common blue violet leaves and blossoms, some chopped clintonia leaves, and a few chopped young orpine leaves. Soft music and candlelight are optional.

EVENING PRIMROSE
Oenothera biennis

Use: Serve roots and young leaves as a cooked vegetable.
Range: Throughout New England
Similarity to toxic species: None
Best time: Very early spring, March and early April
Status: Common and abundant
Tools needed: A hand trowel is useful to dislodge the roots.

The staccato croak of the wood frog rings through my mind every time evening primrose is mentioned. The two go together, because when the first wood frog of the season (wood frogs begin their chorus even earlier than spring peepers) utters its first, raspy note, it is time to dig evening primrose roots.

The evening primrose is biennial, and it is the first year's taproot that foragers seek in early spring. Locate these by first seeking the tall, woody stalks left over from the previous year. The dried seedpods, or capsules, on the old plants are cylindrical in shape. They are reflexed, or scalloped, on the end, evidence of the manner in which the seeds were dispersed. In order to locate the new plants, stand near the old plant and consider the prevailing wind. It is in this direction that the seeds will have fallen, and it is here that the basal rosettes of the young plants will be found.

> FORAGER NOTE: Hold the root under running water and scrub with a clean copper pot scrubber. This is vastly easier than using a knife or potato peeler and saves time and energy when preparing not only evening primrose roots but lots of other root veggies as well.

The young leaves lie flat on the ground, radiating from a central point. They are long and slender, with a pinkish midrib, and are tinged with red on the ends. Later, when spring arrives in earnest, these leaves will stand up and the plant will send forth the young shoot. The time to pick the leaves as a boiling green is when they are still flat on the ground. This season is brief; during a warm spell the plant can become too far gone in only a few days.

Some people enjoy the leaves in a salad, but I prefer to boil them for only five minutes and serve with the usual butter, salt, and pepper. The flavor is sweet and mild. If the leaves are harvested after they stand erect, it may be necessary to use two changes of water.

The roots too are at their best while the leaves are spread flat upon the ground. These can be surprisingly large, as large as the average supermarket carrot. They are creamy white in color, with a top that is approximately the same shade of red as the breast on a rose-breasted grosbeak. Pick as many of the roots as time will permit (don't worry about hurting the stand; they won't be any good next year anyway), take them home, and wash them. They then need to be peeled or scrubbed.

It is never too early in the season for evening primroses. They would be good if taken from under the snow, if they could be located then.

RECIPE

Half-fill a frying pan with water and bring it to a low boil. If the roots are very small, add them whole. Slice medium or large roots lengthwise into two or four pieces. Cook for at least ten minutes. Drain and serve with butter, salt, and pepper. The taste is different from any other root vegetable; it is impossible for me to adequately describe it except to say that it is sweet, mild, and very pleasant.

PINEAPPLE WEED
Matricaria matricarioides

Use: Tea
Range: Throughout New England
Similarity to toxic species: None
Best time: June through October
Status: Common and abundant
Tools needed: None

Once during a plant walk, I pointed to some pineapple weed and asked a lady if she knew what it was. "Sure," she replied, "it's chamomile." She had unwittingly used pineapple weed for the same purpose as chamomile: for colds and as an aid to relaxation.

The chamomile lady was correct in one thing: Pineapple weed is properly utilized as the single ingredient in a mellow, golden, pineapple-scented tea. But tea isn't all this diminutive plant is good for. I like to pick the crumbly flower heads, slightly crush them, and place them in my shirt pocket. The pineapple scent is not pervasive, but it is enough to lift the spirits and brighten the day. Sometimes I chew on the flower heads, just enough to release the delightful pineapple flavor.

Pineapple weed grows abundantly along gravel paths and roads and on gravelly lots. It prefers full sun but can take partial shade. It rarely gets much over 1 foot tall and usually is only 5 or 6 inches high. The feathery leaves resemble those of chamomile, but the flower heads are tightly packed and lack chamomile's white petals. The easiest way to identify this plant is to crush the flower head and sniff it. If it doesn't smell like pineapple, it is the wrong plant.

This pleasant, unassuming little plant offers a sweet fragrance and a satisfying tea. What more could anyone ask?

RECIPE

Pick as many of the greenish-yellow flower heads as patience will allow. Use one teaspoon of dried (the flower heads dry easily for year-round use) or two teaspoons of the fresh flower heads. Cover with boiling water and let them steep for up to five minutes. Sample the tea as is first, then add honey if desired.

COMMON PLANTAIN
Plantago major

Synonym: Plantain
Uses: Cooked vegetable, salad ingredient
Range: Throughout New England
Similarity to toxic species: None
Best time: April and May are best, but new leaves can be harvested throughout the growing season.
Status: Common and abundant
Tools needed: None

What child has not delighted in "shooting" the seeds from the long, thin seed stalk of common plantain? This multifaceted plant thrives in virtually every dooryard in the nation, yet few people recognize its value and worth.

The basal leaves are broad, deeply veined, rounded at the ends, and have wavy margins. The seed heads stand taller than the leaves, which tend to stay close to the ground. The leafstalk has a trough, or groove.

Remedy: *Crushed, the leaves and stalks of common plantain are useful in soothing the sting of rashes, insect bites, and mild burns, including sunburn. Plantain can effectively replace calamine lotion—and it doesn't leave that chalky residue.*

Herbalists use common plantain in an infusion to treat sore throats and coughs, and a decoction of the whole plant is reputed to combat dandruff.

WILD RASPBERRIES AND BLACKBERRIES
Rubus spp.

Uses: Trail nibble, jam or jelly, dessert, tea (leaves), brandy or wine
Range: Throughout New England
Similarity to toxic species: None, although the wilted leaves can be toxic.
Best time: July through September
Status: Common and abundant
Tools needed: None

Wild raspberries are generally smaller and sweeter than the cultivated varieties. Other than that, they are much the same. Wild blackberries are considerably larger than wild raspberries and fill the collecting pail in a shorter time. Both berries are pioneer plants, filling the void when land is clear-cut or burned over.

In years past my fondness for wild raspberries led me to an old farmstead far off the road in a mountainous area of Maine. The berries here were larger than most because they grew in patches in the

FORAGER NOTE: Recipes for raspberry and blackberry jams and jellies are found on the insert that comes with every package of commercially produced pectin. Since the berries lack natural pectin, the store-bought variety is needed to make the jelly set.

middle of large, overgrown fields. Human foragers were not aware of the annual bounty, but the local bears were well informed. They wallowed in the bramble patches, crushing the vines and wreaking havoc in general. A local resident told me that a bear had roused him out of a sound sleep in the wee hours of the morning. It seemed the bruin had become intoxicated on fermented raspberries. The bear staggered, groaned, fell down, and crashed into the side of the man's house before stumbling off into the night. Since ruffed grouse frequently become soused when feeding on apples, why shouldn't the same apply to bears?

FORAGER NOTE: Raspberries and blackberries often grow in such dense colonies that it is impossible to walk through them. It helps to wear a long-sleeved shirt when picking, as well as stout trousers—either canvas or new unwashed (not prewashed) blue jeans. Berry picking can be relaxing work, and the end result more than justifies the effort.

Wild raspberries have round stems, covered with prickly spines. The leaves come in groups of three on adult canes and are compound, with from five to seven leaflets on younger canes. The leaves are wrinkled, roughly toothed, and light colored underneath. Blackberries have long, arched, angled stems with curved spines. The double-toothed leaves are whitish beneath.

FORAGER NOTE: Although wilted raspberry leaves are toxic, the toxin disappears when the leaves are dried completely. Pick a bunch of leaves, dry them, and store them in a closed container for winter use.

Remedy: *Wild raspberry leaves make a pleasant, if somewhat astringent, tea that can be used to treat mild cases of diarrhea. For the strongest medicine, pick the leaves while the plant is in flower. Be sure to use only fresh or dried leaves; wilted leaves are toxic. Blackberry brandy is also used to control diarrhea.*

WILD STRAWBERRY
Fragaria virginiana

Uses: Trail nibble, jam or jelly, dessert
Range: Throughout New England
Similarity to toxic species: None, although the wilted leaves can be toxic
Best time: June
Status: Common and abundant
Tools needed: None

For me, nothing triggers memories of childhood like the fragrance of wild strawberries. Picking these remarkably sweet little berries was one of my favorite youthful pastimes.

Wild strawberries are much smaller than the cultivated kind, but the tame berries don't hold a candle to their diminutive wild cousins when it comes to sweetness.

FORAGER NOTE: As with the fruit of raspberries, blackberries, and other brambles, be sure to use strawberry leaves either fresh or completely dried. The wilted leaf can be toxic.

Wild strawberries grow primarily on poor soil, in full sun or semishade. The leaflets have coarse teeth and prominent veins and grow in groups of three. Wild strawberries and their leaves are a rich source of vitamin C. A strong tea, made by steeping the leaves in boiling water, is a pleasant, vitamin-filled beverage.

FREEZING

To freeze wild strawberries, sprinkle sugar over the berries and stir until they are fully coated. Let the berries sit at room temperature until the sugar combines with the berries to make a syrup, about ten minutes. Place the berries and syrup in a plastic container and freeze immediately. Berries last up to one year in the freezer.

A dish of wild strawberries helps relieve cabin fever during the dark and dreary days of a long New England winter.

Remedy: *Wild strawberry roots were used as toothbrushes by various Native American peoples. The ripe berries too are said to aid in dental hygiene when crushed and rubbed on the teeth and gums. Whether this works or not, it is certainly a pleasant way to begin one of our fleeting, glorious days in June.*

HIGHBUSH CRANBERRY
Viburnum trilobum

Uses: Sauce, jelly
Range: Throughout New England
Similarity to toxic species: None. The nonnative guelder rose (*V. opulus*) looks much like the highbush cranberry. Guelder rose fruit is strong and bitter but not toxic.
Best time: October through early spring
Status: Common and abundant
Tools needed: None

One way to truly appreciate the bounty of nature is to drive around the New England countryside on a sunny October afternoon, picking the fruit of the highbush cranberry. The plant is a member of the honeysuckle family, unrelated to true cranberries. The fruits are often available in startling quantities. A single mile of road in highbush cranberry country could yield thousands of pounds of berries. If not picked by man or bird, the berries persist throughout the winter. Because freezing improves their flavor, the berries can be harvested until the return of warm weather spoils them.

Highbush cranberries grow on tall shrubs rather than vines, as might be expected of something called "cranberry." The coarsely toothed leaves look rather like those of a red maple, with three pointed lobes. The white, rounded flower clusters have smaller flowers in the center, larger ones on the margins. When partially ripe the berries exhibit a striking combination of red and bright yellow. They become completely red when mature. Highbush cranberries are shrubs of the roadsides and hedgerows but sometimes grow along streams and brooks.

For me, highbush cranberries represent the best that a New England autumn has to offer.

RECIPE

To make a cranberry sauce substitute out of highbush cranberries, fill a large saucepan (an enameled seafood steamer works well) with berries; add water just until the top layer of berries floats. Next add the rind of one orange. (The orange rind renders the smelly oils found in the highbush cranberries more tolerable.) Simmer for about five minutes, then mash the cooked berries through a coarse sieve or colander to remove the seeds. Add sugar to taste, along with a package of pectin to make the sauce jell.

The juice can be used alone; just be sure to dilute it with water and add sugar to taste before drinking.

SWEETFERN
Comptonia peregrina

Uses: Tea, stimulant (lively aroma lifts the spirits)
Range: Throughout New England
Similarity to toxic species: None
Best time: June through September
Status: Common and abundant
Tools needed: None

Sweetfern is actually a small shrub in the wax myrtle family. It has woody branches that in late spring sprout fragrant leaves that can be used to make a refreshing tea. The branches too are fragrant and can be picked and sniffed in winter.

RECIPE

A fragrant tea can be made from an infusion of the leaves. This is mostly drunk for pleasure and relaxation, though it was once used medicinally because of its astringent qualities. Sweetfern tea has fallen into disuse for medicinal purposes, but its heady fragrance ranks it as a favorite and beloved tea plant. To make a tea, use one tablespoon of dried leaves or two tablespoons of fresh leaves to one cup of boiling water.

On my various travels around New England over the years, the common sweetfern is like a letter from home. From northern Maine to the White Mountains of New Hampshire and the bustling cities of southern New England, on a rural hillside or in an unused city lot, sweetfern is always present.

My favorite use of sweetfern is to pick the leaves, crush them, and stuff them into my shirt pocket. As I walk, the zesty aroma wafts over me, lifting my spirits, reminding me how great it is to be alive.

Older sweetfern bushes can approach 5 feet in height and twice that in diameter. The slender, segmented leaves resemble fern pinna (the smaller, individual leaflets of a true fern), hence the name sweetfern.

Whether sweetfern was ever used as an oracle is a matter of conjecture. But in the song of the same name by the famous country group the Carter Family, a girl asks the sweetfern if her darling is still true. Perhaps this cosmopolitan shrub has more going for it than we know. It's fun to imagine anyway.

DANDELION
Taraxacum officinale

Synonyms: Spring greens, piss-in-the-bed
Uses: Cooked vegetable, salad, beverage, wine ingredient, medicinal tonic
Range: Throughout New England
Similarity to toxic species: None
Best time: April, May, and October
Status: Abundant; despised as an aggressive weed
Tools needed: An old hunting knife or even a screwdriver may be useful in uprooting dandelions. Inexpensive dandelion diggers are available commercially. Ironically these tools are made specifically to rid lawns of dandelions, so it seems fitting for the forager to use them to harvest dandelions for the table.

When New Englanders say they are going after some greens, they mean dandelions. This European immigrant—brought here purposely, by the way—is firmly entrenched in the culture of the region, both in folklore and in the cuisine of the common people. And now

FORAGER NOTE: Dandelions, or any other wild-food plant, should never be harvested from any lawn where weed killer has been applied.

the lowly dandelion has acquired a distinct air of respectability: It is sold in health food stores and even supermarkets throughout New England.

In my youth a common question in springtime among Maine people was, "Did you have your dandelions yet?" The question presupposed that the person cared enough about dandelions to go out and dig some. This too speaks volumes about how much New Englanders like their dandelions.

Dandelion leaves are deeply lobed, and the hollow stem exudes a milky latex-like liquid when broken. This liquid is one of the bitterest substances imaginable. The golden-yellow blossoms shine in the sun, and each tiny seed is carried on the wind by a white, fluffy "parachute."

The finest dandelions will be found on the edges of lawns and driveways, places where they are not subject to attack from the lawn mower.

Dandelions' medicinal properties have long been known. The scientific name, *Taraxacum officinale,* indicates that the dandelion was once an official plant medicine of the apothecaries, the forerunners of today's druggists. A high vitamin A and C content, plus the presence of vitamins B and D, potassium, iron, and other minerals, explains the dandelion's healthfulness. To this day country people consider the first meal of dandelion leaves, crowns, and buds to be a "tonic," just what the doctor ordered to stimulate a sluggish digestion, improve liver function, and gen-

FORAGER NOTE: In late spring and through the summer, dandelions are too bitter to eat. Basically, as soon as the plants flower, the season is over. But after the first few frosts, the bitter element is mostly dispelled and dandelions are again superb table fare.

erally tone the body and bring it up to snuff. And guess what? The plain old dandelion truly is something of a panacea to the winter-weary body and soul. Folk wisdom, after all, often has some degree of merit.

As early in spring as the dandelions are big enough to spot, they are big enough to pick. Granted, the bigger, fuller dandelions of mid-May provide considerably more substance, but the frail, tender dandelions of early spring are the mildest and, no doubt, most appreciated of all. Dandelion leaves and crowns are wonderful salad ingredients, but my first choice is to use them as boiling greens. Nothing assures me that all is right with the world, that spring has officially arrived, as much as that first steaming-hot mess of cooked dandelions.

FREEZING

Dandelions freeze well, and are superb subjects for the home canner. To freeze, clean and rinse the dandelions. Blanch for two minutes in boiling water. Drain and immediately place in cold water. Drain again and place in freezer bags.

CANNING

Refer to the instructions provided by the canner maker, or call your local Extension Service for tips on canning. In years past dandelions were preserved in yet another way. I learned of this when a friend presented me with a quart of what he called "slack-salted dandelion greens." As he explained it to me, the dandelions were put up in an earthenware crock, a layer of dandelions and a layer of pickling salt, alternating the plants and the salt until the crock was full.

RECIPE

Dig up the dandelions—roots and all if possible. Try to dislodge as much dirt, sand, grit, and earthworms as possible in the field; this will make the final cleaning much easier. Rinse the field-cleaned dandelions, and soak them in a pan of lightly salted water for an hour before using.

The different parts of the plant require different cooking times and methods. Peel, chop, and boil the roots for fifteen minutes. Steam or boil the leaves for at least ten minutes. Boil the crowns, along with any unopened buds, for fifteen minutes. Drain and serve with salt, pepper, butter, and perhaps apple cider vinegar.

GROUND IVY
Glechoma hederacea

Synonyms: Gill-over-the-ground, alehoof
Uses: Tea, bitter tonic
Range: Throughout New England
Similarity to toxic species: None
Best time: April through November
Status: Common weed of lawns and waste places
Tools needed: None

Ground ivy is an attractive ground cover, and it's a mystery to me why more people don't appreciate this low-growing plant, with its hoof-shaped, ruffled leaves and attractive, wee flowers. But ground ivy, despite its good looks and multiple uses, is almost universally reviled as an invasive "weed."

RECIPE

To brew a pleasant, healthful tea, chop a small handful (the amount of plant material can vary, according to taste) of fresh-ground ivy leaves. Place the leaves in a teacup, and pour in boiling water. Let the tea steep for a few minutes. Place a saucer over the teacup to help retain both the heat and the volatile oils of the ground ivy.

A friend has a little wood yard behind his barn, a place where he saws his annual supply of firewood into stove-length sections. Sawdust, wood chips, old asphalt shingles, and rotting pine boards make this a no-man's-land for most plants. That the determined ground ivy thrives here is indicative of its tenacity.

Ground ivy has square stems, which help identify it as one of the mints, even though it lacks the characteristic "minty" aroma. Ground ivy seldom grows more than 5 or 6 inches tall. The rounded leaves are roughly toothed, and the tiny violet-blue flowers grow from the leaf axils.

Remedy: *For use as a bitter tonic, simply refrigerate the tea and sip a few ounces, cold, about twenty minutes before a meal. This tonic helps stimulate the appetite—and in my experience it makes food taste better. Taking bitters before meals was once as common a practice as having a cup of coffee first thing in the morning is today. To my knowledge, only one company currently manufactures bitters, and while these are of good quality, they are expensive. I find it cheaper to make my own bitters, and ground ivy is the main ingredient.*

Remedy: *Ground ivy is rich in vitamin C, which helps explain why it is so useful when given hot to someone with a cold.*

OX-EYE DAISY
Chrysanthemum leucanthemum

Synonym: Daisy
Uses: Trail nibble, salad green
Range: Throughout New England
Similarity to toxic species: None
Best time: May through August
Status: Ubiquitous throughout the region
Tools needed: None

If called to name a common wild-flower, it seems fair to assume that the familiar white-and-yellow daisy of roadsides, fields, vacant lots, and lawns would come first to most people's mind. Who as a child, or even as an adult, has not made a bouquet of daisies for the summertime table? The ox-eye daisy is not a native of North America but rather of Europe.

And yet it has not only totally assimilated into our culture but has become an icon in the process.

Ox-eye daisies are a fine example of a composite flower, with their yellow center disc and white rays, or petals. The flowers measure about 2 inches in diameter. With their snow-white petals and sunny-yellow center disc (compressed in the center), daisy blossoms are hard to mistake. Add the smooth, elongated leaves with their coarse, irregular teeth, or lobes, and identification is complete. Daisies can attain a height of up to 3 feet, but most plants run only about a foot or so.

Given its familiarity to everyone who ever stepped out-of-doors and its universal appeal, it seems strange that more people are unaware that daisies provide some tasty treats. Yes, daisies are edible. So when summer arrives and daisies show up on lawns and along driveways and paths, enjoy the color and beauty, but also be sure to give them a try as another tasty, wild treat.

Trail food: *As readers might have guessed by now, my favorite use of any wild plant is to eat it out of hand. In my estimation the best parts of a daisy are the unopened flower buds, which I just pick and munch on.*

RECIPE

Daisy buds are even better on a wild or simple garden salad. Plain loose-leaf lettuce takes on a new dimension with the addition of a handful of daisy buds.

Chopped daisy leaves also make a wonderful addition to any salad. Surprisingly the leaves have a distinct carroty flavor, which even the most robust salad dressing cannot obscure.

GROUND JUNIPER
Juniperus communis var. *depressa*

Use: Seasoning
Range: Throughout New England
Similarity to toxic species: None
Best time: August through November
Status: Common
Tools needed: Gloves help protect fingers when picking berries, since the leaves (needles) are stiff and very sharp.

When I was a youngster, my grandpa took me with him to hunt snowshoe hares. Often the hares would hide in the vast stands of ground juniper that blanketed the hillsides where we hunted. Grandpa would have me walk

---

RECIPE

Crush the dried berries with a mallet or the handle of a table knife. Sprinkle on roasts (lamb especially benefits from crushed juniper berries), and cook in the normal fashion. Scrape off the berries before serving, since they can be tough and woody.

through the tangled, prickly juniper in order to flush hares out in the open where he could shoot them. At that time it never occurred to me that this tough, prickly, and unyielding shrub had any practical use other than providing a safe haven for hares.

Long after my hunting days with Grandpa, an acquaintance asked me if I used juniper berries in cooking. My reply took the form of a question rather than an answer. When I asked why anyone would even wish to use such a mean and difficult shrub in cooking, I was treated to a brief history of juniper berries in Swedish cuisine.

My friend's wife hails from Sweden, and she had carried much of her culture here to the United States. This included using crushed juniper berries as a flavoring for meats. Shortly after our discussion, my friend's wife sent me a container full of juniper berries. These seemed to me identical in every way to berries found on our native ground juniper.

For anyone who has not had the dubious pleasure of tramping through a ground juniper jungle, look for a low-growing, mostly flattened evergreen shrub with spreading branches and short (½ inch) leaves, or needles. These three-sided leaves are hollow and occur in whorls of three. Berries, which come on in late summer and persist well into winter, begin as a light shade of green and acquire a bluish-black color as they mature.

It's nice to know that this rough-and-tumble plant has a culinary use. It all goes to show that physical appearances can be deceiving.

DRYING

Spread out the berries on a nylon window screen, or even on the bottom of a loosely woven basket, and place them out of direct sunlight to dry. Keep the dried berries in a sealed container. The dried berries have a long shelf life, keeping their aromatic, somewhat resinous taste for some time.

HIGHBUSH BLUEBERRY
Vaccinium spp.

Synonym: Huckleberry
Uses: Trail nibble, jam or jelly, pie filling, muffin ingredient, raw fruit salads, dried
Range: Throughout New England
Similarity to toxic species: May be mistaken for buckthorn (*Rhamnus* ssp.), a cathartic, but buckthorn has long, sharp thorns, and its berries are bitter.
Best time: July and August
Status: Common locally
Tools needed: None

Wild Maine blueberries have a worldwide following. But these are the lowbush variety, and while they are certainly "wild," blueberry growers go to lengths to nurture their crops by burning blueberry fields on alternate years and applying pesticides as needed. It is not only dangerous to pick these (because of the toxic spray used on them) but also usually illegal, since most Maine blueberry fields are commercial and privately owned. Picking berries from these fields is, in fact, stealing.

FORAGER NOTE: Don't wash blueberries if they are to go in the refrigerator or freezer for storage. Doing so will make them mushy and also affect their flavor.

But Maine, indeed all of New England, has another blueberry, this one not cultivated or pampered in any way. Highbush blueberries grow on shrubs, some of which can attain a height of 10 feet or more, and are found in waste places, including overgrown fields and power line rights-of-way, and also along streams and ponds.

Look for these shrubs, many with tightly gathered and often twisted branches, in the places described above. The leaves are of an elliptical shape and may have very fine teeth or no teeth at all. Blueberry blossoms, which form in mid-spring, are white and bell-shaped and resemble the globe on a kerosene lamp. The berries look like, well, blueberries.

> FORAGER NOTE: The only aspect of dealing with blueberries that may take some time is cleaning them. I prefer to spread the berries out on a flat surface. If it's a windy day, I push the berries about so that the wind blows any sticks, leaves, and other debris away. On calm, still days an electric fan or even a magazine, waved about like a handheld fan, serves the same purpose

Trail food: *As far as using wild highbush blueberries goes, eating them out of hand takes first place in my estimation.*

FREEZING

Blueberries last for many weeks in the refrigerator if kept in a sealed container. For long-term storage, the freezing process is simple: Just put the cleaned berries in a container and place the container in the freezer. That's it. No muss, fuss, blanching, or further processing required. I have kept frozen blueberries for two years with no noticeable change in flavor or texture.

RECIPE

Any pie, muffin, or jelly recipe works for highbush blueberries, since they are no different than any other blueberry. Use huckleberries the same as blueberries. Try rolling a scant handful of dry (not dried, but dry, as in not wet) berries in flour and adding to a batch of pancake batter.

NEW ENGLAND ASTER
Aster novae-angliae

Synonym: Aster
Uses: Cut flower
Range: Throughout New England
Similarity to toxic species: None
Best time: Late August through October
Status: Common weed
Tools needed: Knife

Why include something that cannot be eaten in a book about foraging? Because beauty, as exhibited in the showy New England aster, is food for the spirit. What could complement a meal of freshly harvested wild foods better than a freshly picked bouquet of brilliantly colored wildflowers?

The New England aster is an icon of the glory days of late summer and early fall. Here in New England the September air is clean and crisp. Cerulean skies and powder-puff white clouds call for extended walks afield. And to remind us that there is more to life than food, the New England aster brightens our days for a brief, glorious season.

In shades of violet, magenta, pink, and sometimes rose, the New England aster is a pioneer plant. Even the roughest of roadside embankments are quickly colonized by this magnificent wildflower. Disturbed ground and waste places don't stay barren long if New England asters are nearby. The windborne seeds, carried on tiny white "parachutes," find their way to far-off ground to become the crowning beauty of the following season.

New England asters usually grow to about 3 feet tall, but individual plants can reach more than twice that size. The stem is hairy but not prickly. The toothless leaves clasp the stem, which is topped by bunches of daisy-shaped flowers.

Cut asters last for three or four days in a water-filled vase. During the blooming season, not a day passes that my kitchen table is not graced with a colorful bouquet of asters. Fading flowers are immediately replaced from among the wild asters blooming right outside my cottage. Once the nearest asters were miles down the road. A few handfuls of the fluffy seeds, strewn about and carried by the wind, changed that in a hurry. Anybody can do the same. Simply fill a plastic sandwich bag with the seeds and spread them on any waste ground. In time a rough-looking space will become a beautiful wildflower garden.

By October's end the vegetable and flower gardens have succumbed to killing frosts. Foraging, except for animal species, is practically done for the season. To properly complete the annual cycle, a few New England asters tenaciously cling to life for just a few more days.

Animals

New England seashores, lakes, streams, ponds, and wetlands host multiple species of common, easily harvested animals. Many of these, while mostly ignored by anglers and hunters, make superb table fare and are perfect quarry for the recreational forager.

Before harvesting any animal, always consult your state or local regulations.

CRAYFISH
Decapoda astacus

Synonyms: Crawfish, crawdad
Uses: The cooked tails are similar to lobster in flavor and texture; also used as fish bait.
Range: Throughout New England
Similarity to toxic species: None, but the pincers can inflict a painful wound.
Best time: May and June in brooks and streams; May through September in lakes and ponds
Status: Common and abundant
Tools needed: A collecting pail and rubber boots for handpicking. More sophisticated tools include a wire-mesh minnow trap for overnight use in ponds and lakes. A dip net and a bit of fish or chicken tied to string can be useful for collecting during the day.

On Maine's Moosehead Lake, crayfish grow unusually large. Locals know them by the sobriquet *Moosehead lobster*. It isn't unusual to see strings dangling into the water from private docks. These usually have a bit of fish, or perhaps a chicken wing, tied on the end. The camp owner tends these strings regularly, slowly pulling the bait toward the surface. The crayfish clinging to the bait are reluctant to release their grip and can be scooped in with a long-handled dip net.

When enough crayfish are captured, they are steamed until they turn red. Then the tail, the only part worth bothering with, is pulled from the body and its meat is dug out, dipped in melted butter, and consumed with great relish.

My first dish of crayfish was obtained in an amusing way. While I was fishing a local lake, a good-size smallmouth bass hit my lure. When the fish was

Cooking crayfish "New England style" is a breeze. While the famed Louisiana "crawfish boil" requires added spices and considerable fussing, our Eastern method needs only a saucepan and about 2 inches of boiling water. Drop the live crayfish in and cover. Let them cook for perhaps ten minutes, turn off the heat, and remove the crayfish. This method steams rather than boils the crayfish. Boiling is an acceptable method, but it takes longer to heat the water and, at least to my taste, seems to render the crayfish rather bland. Steaming seals in the flavor.

Let the cooked crayfish cool for a few moments, then, while holding the body with one hand, pull the tail away with the other. The small, dark vein on the outside of the tail meat can be discarded and the end of the tail pinched to make the meat pop out. It may be necessary to partially split the shell of the tail in order to remove the meat, using either fingers or a pocketknife (or a fancy steak knife, for the more refined forager). Dip the hot tail meat in melted butter and enjoy.

A mess of steamed crayfish can be the crowning touch to any camping trip. Just don't forget the butter.

netted, a 3-inch-long crayfish popped out of its mouth. The crayfish was still alive; it had evidently only just then been caught by the bass, which in turn was only just then caught by me. Bass and crayfish both went into my cooler, and as a side dish with my bass fillets that evening, I tried my first steamed crayfish. It was delicious, comparable to lobster. Foraging for crayfish immediately became a serious pastime.

The simplest way to catch crayfish is to visit a stream or brook, turn over underwater rocks, and wait for the current to wash away any mud or silt. If a crayfish is present, it will be immediately visible when the water clears, its pincer claws held aloft in a gesture of defiance. The crayfish can then be scooped up in a simple homemade net or taken by hand. The manual method is a challenge. While keeping the animal's attention with one hand (making sure the little critter doesn't grab hold of a finger), slowly move your other hand behind the crayfish—they move backward when frightened—and grasp the body. Plunk the crayfish in a pail and look for another one.

A wire minnow trap is probably a more effective way to capture crayfish. These are cheaply bought or can be made of ¼-inch hardware cloth. The dimensions for this trap are unimportant—they truly depend on how much hardware cloth you have on hand. However, for those who like more precise directions, the trap can be from 1 to 3 feet long and from 8 to 20 inches round. The wire mesh is rolled into any length to form a tube, then two other pieces of mesh are each formed into a funnel shape, the mouths of the funnels measuring the same diameter as the tube. Insert a funnel, narrow end first, into both ends of the tube; use the loose ends of wire to attach the funnels to the tube openings. With wire cutters cut a square from the side of the tube and refasten it loosely. This square is removed to empty the trap once the crayfish enter it.

Bait the trap with any meat, poultry, or fish. Tie the trap to a stout cord, and place it underwater in a shallow section of a pond or lake. It's best to leave the trap overnight and check it the next morning. With luck it will be filled with lively crayfish.

Most people who own small ponds that have become infested with crayfish are only too happy to allow a forager to trap the critters. That's because the crayfish muddy the water by building nests in the banks. Such private ponds can provide a practically endless source of crayfish for the astute forager.

Crayfish are usually dark green in color, although the body can exhibit traces of brown and even tinges of yellow. A detailed description of the physical appearance is unnecessary, because a crayfish resembles a lobster in nearly every way except for size. Aside from the unusually large Moosehead Lake variety, crayfish average about 3 inches long.

BULLFROG
Rana catesbeiana

Use: The skinned, fried legs are considered a delicacy.

Range: Throughout New England; scarce in far northern Maine

Similarity to toxic species: None

Best time: Summer and early fall

Status: Common and abundant throughout their range

Tools needed: You can catch bullfrogs by hand or with a homemade frog spear. A slingshot or a bit of red cloth on a fishhook will also work. Kill bullfrogs by hitting them on the head with a heavy stick or a short bit of metal water pipe.

After I had spoken to a group about frogs, a woman asked me what a female frog is called. She was surprised to learn that the term *bullfrog* refers to a specific species of frog, not to any distinction between the sexes.

Bullfrogs are not the meek, mild creatures they are commonly thought to be. Instead of patiently sitting on lily pads waiting for bugs to pass within grabbing range, bullfrogs are aggressive predators, sometimes even cannibalistic. Their diet includes small mammals, frogs, salamanders, newts, snakes, small turtles, baby birds, spiders, snails, insects, and crayfish.

One summer a horde of bullfrogs arrived at my farm pond. The frogs mostly stayed on a small island in the middle of the pond, pretty much out of sight and out of mind except for the occasional deep, thundering *jug-o'-rum* call. One day I threw some stale bread to the minnows in the pond. Dozens of the little fish soon swirled, feeding heartily. Then a bullfrog jumped into the water and, swimming ever so slowly, positioned itself in the center of the feeding minnows. Suddenly the frog lunged for and captured a minnow. A larger frog, watching from the island, jumped in and quickly approached the first frog. The smaller frog tried to hold its ground but was forced to retreat after the larger animal bit it savagely and repeatedly. The victor claimed rights to the minnows and protected its turf by driving off any other frog that came within range. It's a good thing bullfrogs don't get as large as house cats!

There was scarcely a country boy in days past who had not killed a few bull-frogs and cooked himself a mess of frog legs. In my time, frog hunting was a rite of passage. Perhaps our youthful culinary endeavors were a bit crude, but fancy frog-leg cookery differs little from the primitive method we employed.

Foragers who stick to hunting bullfrogs, which are common and abundant, need not worry unduly about affecting local populations. However, because some frogs (and other amphibians) are becoming scarce or even disappearing, it is worthwhile to study the situation. FrogWatch USA is a program that moni-tors frog activity by assessing data collected by volunteers. The program, which can be joined over the Internet or by phone or mail, assigns observer numbers to volunteers who, during the breeding season, regularly visit vernal pools and wetlands to record what kind of frog calls are heard and the intensity of the calls.

Participation in FrogWatch USA is a wonderful way to involve children in nature firsthand. Adults, me included, benefit too, if only because the monitor-ing sessions are so enjoyable. For more information visit www.aza.org/frogwatch or e-mail frogwatch@aza.org.

RECIPE

To prepare the legs, make a slit around where the thickest part of the leg joins the body. Leaving the legs attached to the frog, grab the skin with pliers and pull toward the feet. With the skin hanging around the feet, cut off the feet and discard skin and feet. With a sharp knife, disjoint the skinned legs where they join the body. Discard the body—there's no meat on it worth bothering about. Roll the legs in flour or cornmeal and pan-fry to a golden brown. Season to taste with salt and pepper.

The discriminating connoisseur of fine foods pays fancy prices for frog legs in posh restaurants. Self-reliant foragers catch and prepare their own frog legs—and don't pay a cent.

COMMON BLUE MUSSEL
Mytilus edulis

Synonyms: Blue mussel, mussel
Uses: Cooked seafood, pickled snack
Range: Throughout coastal New England
Similarity to toxic species: None
Best time: Available year-round
Status: Common and abundant
Tools needed: None

The scientific name for the common blue mussel of the New England seashore reveals its most valuable feature: *Mytilus edulis* means "edible mussel." Mussels

RECIPE

Adding a slight amount of crushed garlic, an ounce of sherry, and some thin-sliced onion to the pot with the fresh mussels imparts a delicate taste to the basic mussel flavor. Amounts of each ingredient are determined according to personal preference. This is my favorite mussel recipe and to me represents the pinnacle of mussel cookery.

were once scorned by New England-ers, taking a backseat to clams and oysters. No longer relegated to obscurity, today the common blue mussel has gained regional acceptance and is a common item on restaurant menus and in the seafood cooler at grocery stores. Mussel farming to produce large, grit-free mussels is a thriving new industry in New England.

But it is the wild variety of the blue mussel that concerns foragers. After periwinkles, mussels are our most abundant shellfish. Compared to digging clams, which is hard labor at best, picking mussels is a walk in the park. Vast colonies of mussels lie exposed each time the tide goes out. It is possible to gather enough for a meal in a matter of minutes.

FORAGER NOTE: Never carry or store mussels submerged in water. I place the mussels in a cooler upon returning to my vehicle from the mussel beds. At home I rinse the mussels again and place them in the refrigerator, where they can be safely stored for several days. They never last that long at my house.

The mussels produce a holdfast, or beard—a tangled mass of threadlike filaments used by the mussel to anchor itself to rocks or even to other mussels. The beard, or byssus, may be removed when the mussel is picked or left on and used to grasp the meat after the mussel is cooked.

Mussel shells range in color from black to navy blue. Each half of the 2- to 3-inch shell is deeply concave. The body of the mussel is generally orange, sometimes turning creamy white when cooked.

Any kind of container may be used to collect mussels, but most serious mussel harvesters prefer wood or wire-mesh clam baskets, or rollers. These can be sloshed in the water to remove any clinging mud or grit from the mussels. For

RECIPE

To steam mussels, place them in a pot, cover, and turn the heat to high. It's that simple. The natural juices contained within the mussel are released within minutes. When the pot bubbles and froth creeps over the edge, set the cover so that the steam can escape, and turn down the heat to medium. Cook until the mussel shells gape open.

To serve, lift the shells out of the pan with a slotted spoon or similar utensil. Drain and reserve the broth, or "nectar," in a small bowl to be used as a final rinse for the mussel meats. Although some like to add melted butter to the nectar, I believe it harms the delicate flavor. The nectar can be drunk at the end of the meal—the crowning touch to a simple but hearty and flavorful meal.

Here is a favorite old-time Downeast recipe that utilizes leftover mussel meats. Here again, amounts of each ingredient are determined according to taste and according to the size of the vessel used.

Begin by picking out the cooked mussel meats from the shells and placing them on a plate. Next slice an onion as thinly as possible. Line the bottom of a clean, screw-top jar with the mussels and top with a layer of onion slices. Keep alternating mussel meats and onion slices until the jar is nearly full. Then tuck several northern bay leaves (don't substitute commercial bay leaves) on the inside of the jar, between the glass and the mussels. Fill the jar to the top with white vinegar, and tap the jar to release any trapped air. Add more vinegar if needed. Allow to stand in the refrigerator for at least three or four days. The pickled mussels will keep in the refrigerator for several weeks.

a cheap and easy substitute, a nylon mesh bag fills the role wonderfully. For the thrifty forager, a secondhand onion bag works just fine. Anything that allows the water to drain is acceptable.

Steamed mussels are not the plebeian fare many might suppose. The key to a memorable meal of steamed mussels is to steam the bivalves in their own juices. It is likely that one of the reasons mussels took so long to gain appreciation from the general public is that most people knew only boiled, rather than steamed, mussels. To place fresh mussels in a great pot of boiling water is a sin. The resulting product tastes like cardboard, with nothing to recommend it except that it contains many vitamins and trace minerals.

Mussels lend themselves to countless recipes. The recipes in this section are only a select few of my favorites. Do delve into the many fascinating ways to use these free gifts of the sea; the experiment can last a lifetime.

The possibilities being endless, my last suggestion is to experiment, experiment. There is no wrong way (except perhaps for boiling) to cook blue mussels!

EXTRA RECIPE

Mussels in pesto are a summertime delight. Steam the mussels, remove the meats, and slather them with room-temperature, homemade pesto. This simple meal can be eaten as is or used to top pasta.

PERIWINKLE
Littorina littorea

Synonym: Wink
Use: Cooked shellfish
Range: Throughout coastal New England
Similarity to toxic species: None
Best time: Year-round
Status: Common and plentiful
Tools needed: None

Common periwinkles are said to grow to 1 inch in diameter, but they're almost always a bit smaller than that. The spiral shells come in various shades of brown and are sometimes

FORAGER NOTE: Although periwinkles appear to be stationary, they are constantly on the move, albeit at a snail's pace.

If enough periwinkles remain after cooking a batch, they may be treated the same as the common blue mussel and pickled in white vinegar. Slice an onion as thinly as possible. Line the bottom of a clean, screw-top jar with the periwinkles and top with a layer of onion slices. Keep alternating periwinkles and onion slices until the jar is nearly full. Then tuck several northern bay leaves (don't substitute commercial bay leaves) on the inside of the jar, between the glass and the periwinkles. Fill the jar to the top with white vinegar, and tap the jar to release any trapped air. Add more vinegar if needed. Allow to stand in the refrigerator for at least three or four days. The pickled periwinkles will keep in the refrigerator for several weeks.

tinged with yellow. Rocks near the high-tide line are covered with these plentiful mollusks.

Although easy to harvest and delicious when boiled, few people bother with periwinkles—probably because, like dandelions, they are too common. Or perhaps nobody knows that periwinkles are eminently edible. For the astute forager, however, periwinkles are a high-priority item.

It is easy to pick periwinkles. Grasp them, pull them from the rock, and drop them in a container. It takes lots to make a meal, so collect at least a pint per person.

Back at home, put the periwinkles in water to make sure they are all alive. (Dead ones will float; live ones sink.) Rinse well and drain. Next boil water in a medium-size saucepan. A few tablespoons of salt added to the water will make the periwinkle meats a bit resilient—all the better for removing them from the spiraled shell. Boil for about five minutes. Be careful not to overcook, which will make the meat tough.

Remove the periwinkles from the water, drain, and place on a serving dish. The meat can be removed from the shell with a toothpick, a nutpick, or even a common finishing nail.

Like the popular commercial snack, it is impossible to "eat just one," but unlike that snack, some time must elapse between mouthfuls of periwinkle. It takes a moment to stab the periwinkle meat and pull it from the shell. Eating periwinkles is definitely a hands-on activity.

When harvesting periwinkles, be prepared to be the subject of odd looks from passersby. It's amusing to imagine what people think when they see a periwinkle harvester. Perhaps they take pity, seeing some poor soul reduced to eating periwinkles. Little do they

FORAGER NOTE: Boiling rather than steaming periwinkles is necessary because boiling introduces the salt to the periwinkle, whereas steaming would not.

know that instead of being a poor tatterdemalion, the forager is taking advantage of one of New England's tastiest seafoods.

ATLANTIC RAZOR CLAM
Ensis directus

Synonym: Razor clam
Use: Used fresh or cooked in a variety of recipes
Range: Throughout coastal New England
Similarity to toxic species: None
Best time: Year-round
Status: Locally abundant
Tools needed: Razor clams can be harvested by hand, but a handheld trowel, a garden spade, or a standard clam hoe will make the process easier.

Many years ago a section of clam flats near my Belfast, Maine, home was opened to harvesting for the first time in twenty-five years. Locals, knowing it held huge surf clams, flocked to the place. Besides surf clams we found vast numbers of razor clams. A big man with a long red

FORAGER NOTE: Razor clams are not sold commercially because they don't keep well. To enjoy the tantalizing, rich flavor of these unique shellfish, you must go out and harvest them yourself.

Small razor clams—no longer than a person's index finger—are excellent raw, although unlike old Red Beard, I like to take them home to prepare and serve them rather than consume them on the beach.

It is easy to open razor clams because they cannot close their shells completely. A sharp knife can lay the shell open, where the meat is easily removed. Place the meats back in the shells and serve on a platter of crushed ice. Finishing touches include a few sprigs of fresh parsley and some lemon wedges, artistically arranged along the edge of the platter. Squeeze a bit of lemon juice on the raw clam, pick it up with a small seafood fork, and enjoy!

Steamed razor clams are superb, rivaling common steamer clams for taste. As with mussels, don't use any water; the razor clams contain more than enough natural juice for steaming. Steam the clams until the shells are completely open and the clam meat has shrunk to about half its raw size. Reserve the broth for dipping and later drinking.

beard sat on a rock and with a jackknife deftly opened one razor clam after another and ate them raw, biting pieces off as one would a pickle.

Cooking razor clams is easy; harvesting them can be tricky. Razor clams are so called because they closely resemble an old-fashioned straight-edged razor. The analogy is made complete by the edges of the shells, which are nearly as sharp as a razor. Be careful when harvesting them.

To find razor clams, walk the clam flats on a low tide—the lower the better. Look for airholes in the sand. Because razor clams can move through the sand at amazingly fast speeds, tread lightly to avoid warning them of your presence. With a clam hoe, a hand trowel, or even a spade, quickly turn over the sand. Even if you don't see a clam, carefully stick a hand in the bottom of the hole. It is possible to grasp the fleeing clam by the end of the shell. Here is where the rash forager can end up with a nasty slice on the fingers, so don't try to pull the clam up immediately. Instead hold on with a steady pressure. Anyone who has ever picked night crawlers will understand the technique. In a few moments the clam will relax its grip and can be easily pulled from the hole.

Clam fritters can be made using any commercially prepared or homemade pancake batter. Add clams and whatever clam juice accompanies them. I like a thin batter, but for a fluffier fritter, use a higher proportion of clams and liquid to batter. You'll need one 8¼ -ounce can of condensed milk, 1½ cups flour, 3 tablespoons baking soda, ¾ teaspoons salt, and one beaten egg. Chop clam meat finely. Sift dry ingredients and add egg, milk, and clams. Mix until moist. Cook in hot fat (375°F) for four minutes.

Each person has his or her own favorite chowder recipe; here is mine. Use a pint of chopped clams. Add from one-half to one pint of the reserved clam juice (both the juice and the chopped clams can be frozen for later use in chowders and other dishes), then add a good handful of chopped onion and one large or two small potatoes, peeled and cubed. Many people add a few small chunks of salt pork to chowders, but I prefer to dispense with that tradition. Do, however, add some freshly ground black pepper.

Next is what separates my chowder from others: Simmer the ingredients for about thirty minutes, never allowing the mixture to boil. Add milk only when everything else is cooked, adding just enough so that the chowder is opaque. Too much milk can drown the flavor of the clams, but when used in limited quantities, it will enhance and contain the flavor. Serve the chowder piping hot, with fresh, hot biscuits.

Lacking tools, razor clams can be taken by inserting your hand in the sand on top of the clam's airhole. But do so cautiously because of the sharp edge of the shell.

Razor clams are up to 7 inches long when mature. They appear brown because their shells are covered with a thin, dark outer layer called the *periostracum*. This coating deteriorates when the clam dies, and the shell returns to its true white color.

The clam moves by means of a long, muscular appendage called a *foot* and can change the shape of the foot at will. To move downward into the sand, the razor clam lengthens the foot until it is quite slender. The long, thin appendage is then thrust as far as possible into the sand. The end of the foot is then formed into a knob, which the clam uses as an anchor. All the clam needs to do now is contract the foot and it can zip through the sand with great speed and ease.

Larger razor clams can be chopped and used in fritters, as baked stuffed clams, and in clam chowder. To make baked stuff clams, grind the clams and use the cleaned shells. Mix the clams with commercially prepared or homemade Italian-style bread crumbs. If the mixture becomes too stiff (when baked, a stiff mixture will be too dry), add some of the reserved clam juice. Next chop a green pepper into small pieces and mix with the clams and crumbs. When the mixture is just stiff enough to hold together, use it to fill a clamshell. Continue filling the clamshells until the clam-crumb mixture is used up. Bake the clams at 350°F for twenty minutes, or until the outside of the mixture is slightly browned.

SURF CLAM
Spisula solidissima

Synonyms: Hen clam, quahog
Uses: Chowder or fritter ingredient, as baked stuffed clams, in homemade clam sauce for pasta. The adductor muscle can be cooked or eaten raw.
Range: Throughout coastal New England
Similarity to toxic species: None
Best time: Throughout the year at very low tide
Status: Common locally
Tools needed: None necessary, but a spading fork or clam hoe is a big help.

Surf clams are one of our largest clams, sometimes reaching 6 or more inches long and 5 inches wide. Where harvesting is permitted (pollution and toxic shellfish poison, the so-called red tide, sometimes cause closures of the clam flats), the daily possession limit is usually

FORAGER NOTE: Tide charts, available from most marine supply stores and at sportfishing stores catering to saltwater anglers, are good sources of information on tides throughout the year. Tides in the negative figures are recommended for harvesting surf clams.

Back home with a fresh bunch of surf clams is where the real work begins. Because these hard-shell clams are difficult to open, many folks like to briefly steam them in a little water to make the clams open their shells. But this method has its faults. As the clam is heated, the clam broth is expelled and diluted with water. The broth is better when undiluted, and I am convinced that steaming toughens the clam. Instead, scrub and rinse the clams and place them on the sideboard of the sink. In time the clams will relax and the shell will open enough for you to get in a knife and, with a twist, open the clam fully.

Try to open each clam over a container so that the valuable clam juice is reserved separately. Then use a knife to remove the adductor muscles—those cylinder-shaped muscles that hold the two sections of the shell together. These can be sautéed in butter, with perhaps some fresh herbs added. Serve immediately, while still hot.

To me these treats are tastier than scallops. Some use the adductor muscles in chowders, but that seems a great waste to me, especially since the rest of the clam is perfectly suited for chowder. The tender, sweet adductor muscles are better put to a higher use.

overly liberal. On the other hand, it might as well be, because these giant clams weigh up fast; few people have the physical stamina to carry a full limit from the clam beds back to their vehicle.

Surf clams have thick shells to cope with the pounding the animals receive from waves. When the clams are alive, the shell is coated with a dark film called the *periostracum*. This is quickly lost when the clam dies. The shells of surf clams litter beaches where the clams live. At one time almost every seaside cottage had a stack of neatly scrubbed surf clam shells that people used as ashtrays. My personal favorite use of the shells, other than in stuffed baked clams, is to throw them in depressions in my gravel driveway, where they act as long-lasting fill that will not wash away.

Surf clams live in areas that are usually covered with water. A normal low tide does not drain far enough for practical surf clam harvesting. It is only during very low tides that the sandbars

FORAGER NOTE: To tell the difference between a surf clam hole and holes made by inedible sand dollars, place a foot on either side of the hole and bounce up and down. A surf clam will expel water through its siphon; a sand dollar won't.

RECIPE

The so-called strips, or lengths of flesh along the inside rim of the shell, along with the foot, require additional processing. Using a sharp knife, slice between the strip and the shell to remove the outer strips. Remove the foot from the body of the clam, rinse, and set aside with the strips. The only thing remaining is what Mainers call the "stomach." This can be sliced open and rinsed, but that is a lot of trouble and hardly worth the effort. Concentrate on the strips and feet instead.

The feet and strips are tough and must be chopped or ground. A sharp knife can be used to chop the clam meat, but it is a tedious process. A hand-powered food grinder set on medium or coarse is perfect. The finished product can be used in several ways.

My favorite method is to grind the clams and use the cleaned shells to make stuffed baked clams. Mix the clams with commercially prepared or homemade Italian-style bread crumbs. If the mixture becomes too stiff (when baked, a stiff mixture will be too dry), add some of the reserved clam juice. Next chop a green pepper into small pieces and mix with the clams and crumbs. When the mixture is just stiff enough to hold together, use it to fill a clamshell. Continue filling the clamshells until the clam-crumb mixture is used up. Bake the clams at 350°F for twenty minutes, or until the outside of the mixture is slightly browned.

and gravel banks so favored by surf clams are exposed. Sometimes a strong onshore wind can back up the tide so that clamming is impeded. Conversely, a run-of-the-mill low tide can be strengthened by an offshore wind to the point that the surf clam beds are exposed.

It is possible to find the holes made by surf clams by snorkeling the shallow water during a normal low tide. But the best way is to go out during the "spring" or "low-drain" tides and walk the beach near the water's edge at the time of extreme low tide. Surf clams make breathing holes in the sand; these are the giveaway to their presence.

FORAGER NOTE: I use a large wire-mesh egg basket to hold my surf clams. I can easily swish the clams around in the water and remove most of the clinging sand particles. Anything will do, though. A large onion bag also works, as does a traditional pack basket.

FORAGER NOTE: The stuffed clamshells can be wrapped in aluminum foil and frozen—my personal, wild version of the TV dinner.

All you need do next is carefully work a spading fork (bare hands can do the trick, but the fork makes things easier) under the clam and turn the sand over. With luck, a huge, dark-brown surf clam will be exposed, its propulsion member, or "foot," wiggling in the air.

EXTRA RECIPE

The chopped or ground clams can also be used in a pasta sauce. To a half pint of clams, add about three tablespoons of olive oil, some freshly chopped garlic, freshly chopped oregano, and a few sprigs of chopped thyme. A couple turns of the pepper grinder over the mixture will introduce the correct amount of black pepper. I like to let this sauce sit in the refrigerator a day before using it to allow the flavors to intermingle. Drizzle the heated sauce (don't boil when heating) over your favorite pasta and enjoy!

EXTRA RECIPE

Clam fritters made with chopped surf clams are delicious. Use any commercially prepared or homemade pancake batter. Add clams and whatever clam juice accompanies them. I like a thin batter, but for a fluffier fritter, use a higher proportion of clams and liquid to batter. You'll need one 8¼-ounce can of condensed milk, 1½ cups flour, 3 tablespoons baking soda, ¾ teaspoons salt, and one beaten egg. Chop clam meat finely. Sift dry ingredients and add egg, milk, and clams. Mix until moist. Cook in hot fat (375°F) for four minutes.

EXTRA RECIPE

See clam chowder recipe on page 223.

GLOSSARY

Alternate. Refers to leaves that are alternately arranged on the stems; can also describe leaves that grow singly on the stem.

Basal rosette. Leaves that radiate from a central point at the base of the stem. Many immature plants that lack other identifiable features are easily recognized by the basal rosette.

Bract. A leaflike object that supports a flower cluster, often mistaken for a flower petal. Bunchberry "petals" are actually bracts.

Branchlet. Shoot growth of the current growing season.

Clasping. Refers to a leaf that has no stalk and clasps the stem.

Frond. A fern leaf.

Leaf. The stalk and blade of hardwood trees or plants; the needles and scales of conifers. Pine needles, therefore, are really pine leaves.

Margin. The outer edge of a leaf.

Midrib. The large middle vein of a leaf.

Node. Where the leaf attaches to the stem. The part of the stem between the leaves is called the *internode.*

Opposite. Refers to leaves that are arranged opposite each other.

Perfoliate. Refers to a leaf that surrounds the stem, making the stem appear to perforate the leaf.

Periostracum. The hard outer covering of the shell of many mollusks.

Petal. An inner part of a flower, often colored.

Petiole. The leafstalk.

Rhizome. The underground stem of perennial plants. These often grow horizontally and close to the surface. Rhizomes are not roots, although they are often confused with roots.

Sessile. Refers to a leaf without a stalk.

Sheath. A node is sheathed when the leaf wraps around the stem at the node. Lady's thumb is a fine example of a sheath.

Shoot. New growth, usually in spring.

Simple. Refers to a leaf that has a single blade (the flat part of the leaf).

Stipe. The stem of a fern frond.

Stipule. What looks like a tiny, immature leaf at the base of the petiole. These protect the developing young leaf and never grow into leaves themselves.

Teeth. The little notches on the edge of a leaf that resemble the teeth on a handsaw. Leaves can be finely or coarsely toothed. Some have no teeth and are described as "entire." Certain leaves—some of the oaks, for instance—are not so much toothed as lobed.

Umbel. A group of flowers or fruit with stalks attached at a common point. This grouping resembles a reflexed umbrella.

Veins. Small avenues radiating from the leafstalk, like capillaries in the human body. The plant's sap, with its minerals, water, and various compounds, flows in and out of the veins.

Venation pattern. The way in which the veins are arranged on a leaf. Some are parallel, others pinnate—that is, smaller veins branch from a central, larger main vein.

Wavy. Refers to a leaf margin that is smooth but undulating.

Whorl. Two or more leaves originating at the same level on a common axis.

INDEX

ABOUT THE AUTHOR

Tom Seymour is a freelance journalist, columnist, book author, musician, Maine guide, water dowser, and naturalist. He writes regular features, including a Maine wildlife column, for *The Maine Sportsman,* Maine's largest outdoor publication. Tom also writes an award-winning outdoor/nature column for *The Republican Journal* and front-page features for *Fisherman's Voice* magazine.

Tom's book credits include *Hiking Maine, Fishing Maine,* and *Birding Maine,* all FalconGuides. He also revises *Maine Off The Beaten Path.* Additionally, Tom wrote *Tom Seymour's Maine: A Maine Anthology* and *Hidden World Revealed.* He regularly hosts wild-plant walks in and around Waldo County. He lives in Waldo, Maine.